How to Get Rich Doing Business in Turkey

Turkey Business Guide and Contacts

By

Patrick W. Nee

The Internationalist
www.internationalist.com

Other Titles Featured in the Business Guides Series

MAKING MONEY IN CHINA: Key Business Contacts and Addresses

MAKING MONEY IN CHINA: China Business Guide and Contacts

MAKING MONEY IN CHINA: China Country Guide for Businesses

MAKING MONEY IN RUSSIA: Russia Country Guide for Businesses

MAKING MONEY IN EXPORTING: A Complete Guide to the Business of Exporting

MAKING MONEY IN Brazil: Brazil Business Guide and Contacts

The Internationalist®

International Business, Investment, and Travel

Published by:
The Internationalist Publishing Company
96 Walter Street/Suite 200
Boston MA 02131, USA
Tel: 617-354-7722
www.internationalist.com
PN@internationalist.com

Copyright © 2014 by PWN

The Internationalist is a Registered Trademark. The Making Money series and The Internationalist Business Guides series are Trademarks of the Internationalist Publishing Company.

All rights are reserved under International, Pan-American, and Pan-Asian Conventions. No part of this book may be reproduced in any form without the written permission of the publisher. All rights vigorously enforced.

Welcome to the **Internationalist Business Guides** series:

The key to a successful business is knowing the markets. HOW TO GET RICH DOING BUSINESS IN TURKEY: TURKEY BUSINESS GUIDE AND CONTACTS offers executives, investors, and entrepreneurs the need-to-know information about doing business in Turkey.

Written as an in-depth, straightforward reference guide, this book lists key information about the Turkish market, its challenges, and opportunities. It then looks into a dozen of Turkey's leading industries, their backgrounds, current situation, and projected course.

Whether you are looking to break into international business or need to update your knowledge on Turkish markets— this comprehensive guide is for you.

The Internationalist

Contents

Chapter 1: Country Overview
- Key Leaders
- Geography
- Economy
- Foreign Relations
- U.S.- Turkey Relations
- Principal U.S. Officials

Chapter 2: Economy
- Market Overview
- Market Challenges
- Market Opportunities
- Market Entry Strategy
- Economic Background

Chapter 3: Market Features and Opportunities
- Unique Geographic Location
- Huge and Growing Domestic Market
- EU Customs Union and Accession Partnership
- Black Sea Economic Co-operation
- Openness to Global Trade and Investment

Chapter 4: Energy Efficiency Projects
- Background
- Technical Assessments
- Energy Efficiency Upgrades
- Results
- Project Timeline

Chapter 5: Business Organizations
- Turkish World Business Council

Turkish- American Business Council

Chapter 6: Business Service Providers

Accounting, Auditing, and Tax Services

Banking and Financial Services

Building and Construction Services

Business Management Services

Business Associations

Business Consulting

Car Services and Rentals

Customs Brokerage

Debt Collection

Education and Training Services

Engineering Services

Export Management

Hospitals, Clinics, and Health Services

Human Resources

Legal Services

Debt Collection.

Market Research

Marketing, Public Relations, and Sales

Mining, Oil, and Gas Services

Real Estate Services

Translation and Interpretation

Chapter 1: Country Overview

Key Leaders

Pres.: Abdullah GUL

Prime Min.: Recep Tayyip ERDOGAN

Dep. Prime Min.: Bulent ARINC

Dep. Prime Min.: Besir ATALAY

Dep. Prime Min.: Ali BABACAN

Dep. Prime Min.: Emrullah ISLER

Min. of Agriculture, Food, & Animal Breedi: Mehmet Mehdi EKER

Min. of Culture & Touris: Omer CELIK

Min. of Customs & Trade: Hayati YAZICI

Min. of Development: Cevdet YILMAZ

Min. of Economy: Nihat ZEYBEKCI

Min. of Energy & Natural Resources: Taner YILDIZ

Min. of Environment & Urbanization: Idris GULLUCE

Min. of EU Affairs & Chief Negotiat: Mevlut CAVUSOGLU

Min. of Family & Social Policies: Aysenur ISLAM

Min. of Finan: Mehmet SIMSEK

Min. of Foreign Affairs: Ahmet DAVUTOGLU

Min. of Forestry & Water Works: Veysel EROGLU

Min. of Heal: Mehmet MUEZZINOGLU

Min. of Interior: Efkan ALA

Min. of Justice: Bekir BOZDAG

Min. of Labor & Social Security: Faruk CELIK

Min. of National Defense: Ismet YILMAZ

Min. of National Education: Nabi AVCI

Min. of Science, Industry, & Technology: Fikri ISIK

Min. of Transport, Maritime Affairs, & Communications: Lutfi ELV

Min. of Youth & Sports: Akif Cagatay KILIC

Governor, Central Bank: Erdem BASCI

Ambassador to the US: Namik TAN

Permanent Representative to the UN, New York: Yasar Halit CEVIK

Geography

Area: 780,580 sq. km.

Cities: *Capital*--Ankara (pop. 4.77 million). *Other cities*--Istanbul (13.256 million), Izmir (3.949 million), Bursa (2.605 million), Adana (2.085 million), Gaziantep (1.701 million).

Terrain: Narrow coastal plain surrounds Anatolia, an inland plateau becomes increasingly rugged as it progresses eastward. Turkey includes one of the more earthquake-prone areas of the world.

Climate: Moderate in coastal areas, harsher temperatures inland.

People

Modern Turkey encompasses bustling cosmopolitan centers, pastoral farming villages, barren wastelands, peaceful Aegean coastlines, and steep mountain regions. More than 70% of Turkey's population lives in urban areas that juxtapose Western lifestyles with more traditional ways of life.

The Turkish state has been officially secular since 1924. Approximately 99% of the population is Muslim. Most Turkish Muslims follow the Sunni traditions of Islam, although a significant number follow Alevi and Shiite traditions. Questions regarding the role of religion in society and government, the role of linguistic and ethnic identity, and the public's expectation to live in security dominate public discourse. There are at least 12 million Turkish citizens who assert a Kurdish identity, making them the largest ethnic minority in Turkey.

Nationality: *Noun*--Turk(s). *Adjective*--Turkish.

Population (December 2010 estimate): 73.7 million.
Annual population growth rate (2010 estimate): 1.312%.

Ethnic groups: Turkish, Kurdish, other.

Religions: Muslim 99% (majority Sunni), Christian, Bahai, and Jewish.

Languages: Turkish (official), Kurdish, Arabic, Armenian, Greek.

Education: *Years compulsory*--8. *Attendance*--97.6%. *Literacy*--87.4%.

Health: *Infant mortality rate*--23.94/1,000. *Life expectancy*--72.5 yrs.

Work force (27.43 million): *By occupation*--services 47.1%;

agriculture 26.5%; industry 18.9%; and construction 7.5%.

Government

Type: Republic.

Independence: October 29, 1923.

Constitution: November 7, 1982. Amended in 1987, 1995, 2001, 2007, and 2010.

Branches:
Executive--president (chief of state), prime minister (head of government), Council of Ministers (cabinet--appointed by the president on the nomination of the prime minister).
Legislative--Grand National Assembly (550 members) chosen by national elections at least every 4 years.
Judicial--Constitutional Court, Court of Cassation, Council of State, and other courts.

Political parties with representatives in Parliament: Justice and Development Party (AKP) (327 seats), Republican People's Party (CHP) (135 seats), Nationalist Action Party (MHP) (52 seats), Peace and Democracy Party (BDP) (29 seats), and seven independents.

Suffrage: Universal, 18 and older.

National holiday: Republic Day, October 28-29.

Economy

GDP (nominal): (2005) $481.5 billion; (2006) $526.4 billion; (2007) $658.8 billion; (2008) $680 billion; (2009) $618 billion; (2010) $734.6 billion; (2011 estimated) $789.7 billion.

Annual real GDP growth rate: (2005) 8.4%; (2006) 6.9%; (2007) 4.5%; (2008) 1.1%; (2009) -4.7%; (2010) 9%; (2011 estimated) 47.5%.

GDP (nominal) per capita: (2005) $7,108; (2006) $7,766; (2007) $9,422; (2008) $10,484; (2009) $8,711; (2010) $10,297; (2011 estimated) $11,054.

Annual inflation rate/CPI: (2005) 7.7%; (2006) 9.7%; (2007) 8.4%; (2008) 10.1%; (2009) 6.5%; (2010) 6.4%; (2011 estimated) 9.5%.

Natural resources: Coal, chromium, mercury, copper, boron, Agriculture (9.3% of GDP): *Major products* (CIA World Factbook)--tobacco, cotton, grain, olives, sugar beets, hazelnuts, pulse, citrus; livestock. Provides about 26.5% of jobs (2011) and 3.5% of exports (Jan.-July 2011).

Industry (25.6% of GDP): *Major growth sector, types*--automotive, electronics, food processing, textiles, basic metals, chemicals, and petrochemicals. Provides about 18.9% of jobs and 93.8% of exports.

Trade:
Exports (merchandise)--(2005) $73.5 billion; (2006) $85.5 billion; (2007) $107.2 billion; (2008) $132 billion; (2009) $102.1 billion; (2010) $113.9 billion; (2011 estimated) $141.5 billion.

Export types (Turkish Statistical Institute, 2011)--textiles and apparel, industrial machinery, iron and steel, electronics, petroleum products, and motor vehicles.

Imports (merchandise)--(2005) $116.8 billion; (2006) $139.6 billion; (2007) $170.1 billion; (2008) $201.8 billion; (2009) $140.4 billion; (2010) $185.9 billion; (2011 estimated) $233.7 billion.

Import types--chemicals, petroleum, machinery, motor vehicles, electronics, iron, steel, plastics, precious metals. *Major partners*--Germany, U.S., Italy, France, Russia, Japan, China, Iran, Iraq, U.K.

History

Mustafa Kemal, celebrated by the Turkish State as a Turkish World War I hero and later known as "Ataturk" or "father of the Turks," led the founding of the Republic of Turkey in 1923 after the collapse of the 600-year-old Ottoman Empire and a 3-year war of independence. The empire, which at its peak controlled vast stretches of northern Africa, southeastern Europe, and western Asia, had failed to keep pace with European social and technological developments. The rise of national consciousness impelled several national groups within the Empire to seek independence as nation-states, leading to the empire's fragmentation. This process culminated in the disastrous Ottoman participation in World War I as a German ally. Defeated, shorn of much of its former territory, and partly occupied by forces of the victorious European states, the Ottoman structure was repudiated by Turkish nationalists brought together under the leadership of Mustafa Kemal. The nationalists expelled invading Greek, Russian, French and Italian forces from Anatolia in a bitter war. After the proclamation of the Republic of Turkey the sultanate and caliphate were abolished.

The leaders of the new republic concentrated on consolidating their power and modernizing and Westernizing what had been the empire's core--Asian Anatolia and a part of European Thrace. Social, political, linguistic, and economic reforms and attitudes decreed by Ataturk from 1924-1934 continue to be referred to as the ideological base of modern Turkey. In the post-Ataturk era, and especially after the military coup of 1960, this ideology came to be known as "Kemalism" and his reforms began to be referred to as "revolutions." The core elements of Kemalism are secularism, nationalism, statism, and identification with Europe. All of these concepts are the subject of lively debate in today's Turkey, and the ruling Justice and Development Party (AKP) comes from a tradition that challenges many of the Kemalist precepts.

Turkey entered World War II on the Allied side shortly before the war ended, becoming a charter member of the United Nations. Difficulties faced by Greece after World War II in quelling a communist rebellion and demands by the Soviet Union for military bases in the Turkish Straits prompted the United States to declare the Truman Doctrine in 1947. The doctrine enunciated American intentions to guarantee the security of Turkey and Greece and resulted in large scale U.S. military and economic aid under the Marshall Plan. After participating with United Nations forces in the Korean conflict, Turkey in 1952 joined the North Atlantic Treaty Organization

(NATO). Turkey is currently a European Union candidate.

Political Conditions

The 1982 Constitution, drafted by the military in the wake of a 1980 military coup, proclaims Turkey's system of government as democratic, secular, and parliamentary. The prime minister serves as head of government, and the president serves as head of state. The current president, Abdullah Gul, was elected by Parliament in August 2007 for a 7-year term. Pursuant to a constitutional amendment package approved by voters in an October 2007 referendum, the president is directly elected by the voters for a term of 5 years and can serve for a maximum of two terms.

The 550-member Parliament carries out legislative functions. Pursuant to the October 2007 constitutional amendment package, members of Parliament are directly elected by the voters for a term of 4 years, although general elections may be called at any time. Seat distribution is by the D'Hondt system of party-list proportional representation in combination with a 10% popular vote threshold. To participate in the distribution of seats, a party must obtain at least 10% of the votes cast at the national level. The president enacts laws passed by Parliament within 15 days. With the exception of budgetary laws, the president may return a law to the Parliament for reconsideration. If Parliament reenacts the law, it is binding, although the president may then apply to the Constitutional Court for a reversal of the law. Constitutional amendments pass with a 60% vote, but require an additional popular referendum unless passed with a two-thirds majority.

The president may also submit amendments passed with a two-thirds majority to a popular referendum.

Nationwide local elections for provincial general assemblies, municipal assemblies, and mayoral positions were held March 29, 2009. The AKP received 38.39% of the votes in provincial general assemblies and a similar percentage in municipal assemblies. The Republican People's Party (CHP) and the Nationalist Action Party (MHP) won, respectively, 23% and 15% of the votes. AKP won 10 of 16 metropolitan municipality mayoralties. The next local elections are scheduled for March 2013.

In the June 2011 parliamentary election for Turkey's 61st government, the AKP captured 49.9% of the total votes, and Recep Tayyip Erdogan became the Prime Minister of a single-party government for a third consecutive term. The CHP, led by Kemal Kilicdaroglu, won 25.9% of the vote. The MHP, led by Devlet Bahceli, garnered 12.9% of the vote. Candidates running as independents but affiliated with a voting bloc supported by the Peace and Democracy Party (BDP) earned 6.8% of the popular vote, to encumber 29 seats in Parliament. The next general elections will occur in or before June 2015.

The Judiciary
The judiciary is declared to be independent, but the need for judicial reform and confirmation of its independence are subjects of open debate. Internationally recognized human rights, including freedom of thought, expression, assembly, and travel, are officially enshrined in the Constitution but have at times been

narrowly interpreted, can be limited in times of emergency, and cannot be used to violate what the Constitution and the courts consider the integrity of the state or to impose a system of government based on religion, ethnicity, or the domination of one social class. The Constitution prohibits torture or ill treatment; the current government has focused on ensuring that practice matches principle. The law provides most but not all workers with the right to associate and form unions, subject to diverse restrictions.

The high court system includes a Constitutional Court responsible for judicial review of legislation, a Court of Cassation (or Supreme Court of Appeals), a Council of State serving as the high administrative and appeals court, a Court of Accounts, and a Military Court of Appeals. The High Council of Judges and Prosecutors, appointed by the president, supervises the judiciary.

Principal Government Officials
President of the Republic--Abdullah Gul Prime Minister--Recep Tayyip Erdogan Minister of Foreign Affairs--Ahmet Davutoglu Ambassador to the United States--Namik Tan Ambassador to the United Nations--Ertugrul Apakan.

Turkey maintains an embassy in the United States at:
2525 Massachusetts Avenue
NW, Washington, DC 20008
tel. (202) 612-6700.

Consulates general:

360 N. Michigan Ave., Suite 1405
Chicago, IL 60601
tel: 312-263-0644, ext. 28

4801 Wilshire Blvd., Suite 310
Los Angeles, CA 90010
tel: 323-937-0118

New York
821 United Nations Plaza
New York, NY 10017
tel: 212-949-0160

1990 Post Oak Blvd., Suite 1300
Houston, TX 77056
tel: 713-622-5849

The Permanent Representative of Turkey to the United Nations
821 United Nations Plaza, 10th floor
New York, NY 10017
tel: 212-949-0150

Economy

Turkey is a large, middle-income country with relatively few natural resources. Its economy is currently in transition from a high degree of reliance on agriculture and heavy industry to a more diversified economy with an increasingly large and globalized services sector. Coming out of a tradition of a state-directed economy that was relatively closed to the outside world, Prime Minister and then President Turgut Ozal began to open up the economy in the 1980s, leading to the signing of a customs union with the European Union in 1995. In the 1990s, Turkey's economy suffered from a series of coalition governments with weak economic policies, leading to high-inflation boom-and-bust cycles that culminated in a severe banking and economic crisis in 2001, a deep economic downturn (GNP fell 9.5% in 2001), and an increase in unemployment. Turkey's economy recovered strongly from the 2001 recession thanks to good monetary and fiscal policies and structural economic reforms made with the support of the International Monetary Fund and the World Bank.

Turkey's economy grew an average of 6.0% per year from 2002 through 2007--one of the highest sustained rates of growth in the world. During this period, inflation and interest rates fell significantly, the currency stabilized, and government debt declined to more supportable levels (39.5% of GDP in 2008). However, booming economic growth contributed to a growing current account deficit (5.6% of GDP or $41.6 billion in 2008). Growth fell to 1.1% in 2008, and the economy contracted by 4.7% in 2009 due to the global economic slowdown and reduced exports. Growth picked up to 9% in 2010 and an estimated 7.5% in 2011. Continued implementation of reforms, including tight fiscal policy, and securing independent Central Bank monetary policies is essential to sustain growth and stability.

After years of low levels of foreign direct investment (FDI), Turkey succeeded in attracting $18.3 billion in net FDI in 2008. Global market conditions reduced foreign capital inflows in 2009. Turkey attracted $7.7 billion in net FDI in 2009. Inward FDI increased in 2010 to $9 billion. A series of large privatizations, the stability fostered by the start of Turkey's EU accession negotiations, strong and stable growth, and structural changes in the banking, retail, and telecommunications sectors contributed to the 2008 rise in foreign investment. Turkey has taken steps to improve its investment climate through administrative streamlining, an end to foreign investment screening, and strengthened intellectual property legislation. However, a number of disputes involving foreign investors in Turkey and certain policies, such as high taxation and continuing gaps in the intellectual property regime, inhibit investment. Turkey has a number of bilateral investment and tax treaties, including with the United States, which guarantee free repatriation of capital in convertible currencies and eliminate double taxation.

While Turkey's long-term economic prospects are bright, the government is working to limit growth of its current account deficit, which grew to 10% of GDP in 2011; and rein in inflation of nearly 10%.

EU Accession

Turkey adopted the EU's Common External Tariff regime in 1963, effectively lowering Turkey's tariffs for third countries, including the United States. Turkey and the then-European Economic Community (EEC) entered into an Association Agreement in December 1964. Turkey and the EU also formed a customs union beginning January 1, 1996. The agreement covers industrial and processed agricultural goods and has prompted Turkey to harmonize its laws and regulations with EU standards. In 1999 the European Council granted the status of candidate country to Turkey, and accession negotiations with Turkey were opened in October 2005.

Accession talks include a process of adopting the body of EU law called the *acquis communautaire*. The *acquis* is divided into 33 chapters regulating areas ranging from the free movement of goods to agriculture to competition policy.

As of late November 2010, Turkey had met the benchmarks to open 13 chapters, including the provisionally closed chapter on Science and Research. Most recently, in June 2010, the chapter on Food Safety, Veterinary & Phytosanitary Policy was opened. Eighteen chapters are blocked. Three chapters remain unblocked and have yet to be opened. One of the key stumbling blocks to opening new chapters is that Turkey has yet to fully implement the Ankara Protocol, which requires normalizing bilateral relations with EU member Cyprus, which Turkey has said it will not do until the Greek and Turkish Cypriot communities on the island are reunited.

Energy

In 2010, total electricity supply in Turkey reached 194 terawatt-hours (TWh), up by 51% from 2000. Natural gas fueled 49% of power generation, while coal provided 28%, hydropower 19%, oil 3%, and other sources 1%. Electricity demand in Turkey continues at an annual growth rate of between 6.5% and 8% per year. This, combined with the lack of investment in the sector, mainly due to the Government of Turkey's (GOT) control over prices and slow progress in market liberalization, increased concerns regarding electricity shortages. Official data indicated that Turkey would face electricity shortages as of 2009; however, the GOT revised its projections after experiencing reductions in demand in late 2008, and, due to the global economic crisis and relatively mild weather, Turkey was able to meet its demand. The Ministry of Energy declared a 4.5% annual growth in electricity demand in 2009, half the amount of demand growth in previous years. In 2008, the GOT passed new legislation to encourage investment in the sector, which introduced incentives for companies bringing their facilities online by 2012. Turkey is currently undertaking privatization of its electricity distribution. The private sector has responded, adding 6,644 megawatts (MW) of electricity generation capacity since 2009.

In 2009, fossil fuels accounted for 89% of total primary energy supply (TPES) in Turkey. Coal and natural gas each provided 31% of the total, and oil provided 27%, while renewable energy sources provided the remaining 11%. In 2011, on an energy basis, coal and lignite provided 31% of total final consumption, natural gas 31%, oil 27%, and renewable (biomass, hydro, and geothermal) 11%. Coal is the only energy source with significant domestic availability; over 90% of both oil and natural gas is imported. Domestic oil and gas production is mostly from small fields in the southeast, although major exploration projects are active in the Black Sea. TUPRAS, the largest refiner in Turkey, was privatized in 2005. Turkey has a refining capacity of 714,275 barrels per day (b/d).

Turkey acts as an important link in the East-West Southern Energy Corridor bringing Caspian, Central Asian, and Middle Eastern energy to Europe and world markets. The Baku-Tbilisi-

Ceyhan pipeline, which came online in July 2006, delivers up to 1 million barrels/day of petroleum, and in 2007, the South Caucasus Pipeline (from Shah Deniz) started bringing natural gas from Azerbaijan to Turkey. Turkey's interconnector pipeline to Greece, an important step in bringing Caspian natural gas to Europe via Turkey, came online in November 2007. In July 2009, Turkey signed the Nabucco Intergovernmental Agreement, along with Austria, Bulgaria, Romania, and Hungary, which includes plans for a 2,000-mile natural gas pipeline running from Erzurum, Turkey to Baumgarten, Austria with a 31 billion cubic meter capacity. Alternative proposals to Nabucco include the Trans-Adriatic Pipeline (TAP) and the Italy-Turkey-Greece Interconnector.

Telecommunications

Parliament enacted legislation separating telecommunications policy and regulatory functions in January 2000, by establishing an independent regulatory body, the Telecommunication Authority. The authority is responsible for issuing licenses, supervising operators, and taking necessary technical measures against violations of the rules. Most regulatory functions of the Transport Ministry were transferred to the authority, and the regulator is slowly gaining competence and independence. The Electronic Communication Law passed in 2008 gave greater autonomy to the Telecommunication Authority. The authority realized some important projects in 2008. Introduction of number portability was a big step forward, encouraging more competition among the GSM mobile phone operators. The authority also held a 3G license tender in 2008, where all the

GSM operators participated and started implementing this new technology in Turkey.

The long-expected privatization of the state-owned fixed-line telecommunications company was accomplished by the sale of 55% of Turk Telekom to the Saudi-owned Oger Group in November 2005. The company remains as a monopoly in fixed lines, but the GSM operators' competition against Turk Telekom has been increasing. With liberalization and growth in the economy, there is growing competition for Internet provision, but Turk Telekom remains the sole provider of ADSL wide band Internet.

Environment

With the establishment of the Environment Ministry in 1991, Turkey began to make significant progress addressing its most pressing environmental problems. The most dramatic improvements were significant reductions of air pollution in Istanbul and Ankara. However, progress has been slow on the remaining--and serious--environmental challenges facing Turkey.

In 2011, the Ministry of Environment and Forestry was split into the Ministry of Environment and Urbanization and the Ministry of Forest and Water Affairs. With its goal to join the EU, Turkey has made commendable progress in updating and modernizing its environmental legislation. However, environmental concerns are not fully integrated into public decision-making and enforcement can be weak. Turkey faces a backlog of environmental problems, requiring enormous outlays for infrastructure. The most pressing needs are for water treatment plants, wastewater treatment facilities, solid waste management, and conservation of biodiversity. The discovery of a number of chemical waste sites in 2006 has highlighted weakness in environmental law and oversight.

After long years of silence, Turkey signed the Kyoto Protocol in 2008 and ratified it in 2009. Turkey will not be obligated to reduce its greenhouse emissions until 2012, when the agreement's second commitment period may go into force.

Transport

The Turkish Government gives special priority to major infrastructure projects, especially in the transport sector. The government is in the process of building new airports and highways, thanks to an increased public investment budget. The government will realize many of these projects by utilizing the build-operate-transfer (BOT) model.

Foreign Relations

Turkey is a member of NATO and candidate for the EU, and its primary political, economic, and security ties are with the West. However, the AKP government has also sought to strengthen relations with its Middle Eastern neighbors, and with Central Asian, African, and Latin American countries.

Turkey entered NATO in 1952 and serves as the organization's vital eastern anchor, as it controls the straits leading from the Black Sea to the Aegean and shares a border with Syria, Iraq, and Iran. NATO's Air Component Command Headquarters is located in Izmir and NATO's Rapid Deployable Corps-Turkey is headquartered in Istanbul. As part of NATO command structure reforms, the headquarters in Izmir will transform into the new NATO Land Forces Command headquarters in 2012. Turkey has made important contributions to the International Security Assistance Force (ISAF) in Afghanistan, commanding ISAF four times (2002, 2005, 2009-2010, and 2010-2011). Turkey currently commands Regional Command Capital and has set up two Provincial Reconstruction Teams, in Wardak and Jowzjan Provinces, with approximately 1,700 troops stationed in Afghanistan. Turkey also provides approximately 400 troops to the NATO mission in Kosovo. In Libya, Turkey played an active role in NATO's Operation Unified Protector to protect civilians in 2011. Turkey agreed in 2011 to host a radar as part of NATO's missile defense architecture.

Turkey and the EU formed a customs union beginning January 1, 1996. In December 1999, Turkey became a candidate for EU membership. On December 17, 2004, the EU decided to begin formal accession negotiations with Turkey in October 2005. Besides its relationships with NATO and the EU, Turkey is a member of the Organization for Economic Cooperation and Development (OECD), the Council of Europe, and the Organization for Security and Cooperation in Europe (OSCE).

Turkey is a member of the World Trade Organization (WTO). It has signed free trade agreements with the European Free Trade Association (EFTA), Israel, and many other countries. In 1992, Turkey and 10 other regional nations formed the Black Sea Economic Cooperation (BSEC) Council to expand regional trade and economic cooperation. Turkey chaired BSEC in 2007 and hosted the 15th BSEC Summit in Istanbul in June 2007 and the 17th BSEC Council of Foreign Ministers in Ankara in October 2007. It also belongs to the Organization of Islamic Cooperation (OIC).

Turkey is a UN member and held a non-permanent seat on the Security Council from January 1, 2009 to December 31, 2010. It held the rotating presidency in June 2009 and September 2010. In May 2011, Turkey announced its candidacy for a non-permanent seat for 2015-2016.

U.S.- Turkey Relations

U.S.-Turkish friendship dates to the late 18th century and was officially sealed by a treaty in 1830. The present close relationship began with the agreement of July 12, 1947, which implemented the Truman Doctrine. As part of the cooperative effort to further Turkish economic and military self-reliance, the United States has loaned and granted Turkey more than $7 billion in economic aid and more than $14 billion in military assistance over several years.

U.S.-Turkish relations focus on areas such as strategic energy cooperation, trade and investment, security ties, regional stability, counterterrorism, and human rights progress. Relations were strained when Turkey refused in March 2003 to allow U.S. troops to deploy through its territory to Iraq in Operation Iraqi Freedom, but regained momentum steadily thereafter, and mutual interests remain strong across a wide spectrum of issues. Turkey currently allows the use of Incirlik Air Base for the transport of non-lethal cargo in support of Operation Enduring

Freedom and Operation Iraqi Freedom. On July 5, 2006, Secretary of State Condoleezza Rice and Foreign Minister Abdullah Gul signed a Shared Vision Statement to highlight the common values and goals between the two countries and to lay out a framework for increased strategic dialogue. During a November 5, 2007 meeting in Washington with Prime Minister Erdogan, President George W. Bush committed to provide greater assistance to Turkey in its fight against terrorism from the Kurdistan Workers' Party (PKK or Kongra Gel), which he characterized as a "common enemy" of Turkey, Iraq, and the United States. He reiterated this commitment during President Gul's January 8, 2008, White House visit.

President Barack Obama paid a historic visit to Turkey April 5-7, 2009, the first bilateral visit of his presidency. During the visit, he spoke before the Turkish Parliament and outlined his vision of a model U.S.-Turkish partnership based on mutual interests and mutual respect. Secretary of State Hillary Clinton has also prioritized the U.S.-Turkey relationship, and visited Turkey in March 2009 and July 2011. On December 7, 2009, Prime Minister Erdogan and President Obama launched the Framework for Strategic Economic and Commercial Cooperation (FSECC), a new cabinet-level initiative focused on boosting trade and investment ties. The inaugural FSECC meeting was held in Washington in October 2010. In addition to the new framework, the U.S. and Turkey hold meetings of the Trade and Investment Framework Agreement (TIFA) Council and Economic Partnership Commission (EPC). In 2011, bilateral trade reached record levels, increasing by 35% year on year from $14.8 billion to $19.9 billion, with U.S. exports to Turkey up 39% from $10.5

billion to $14.6 billion and Turkish exports to the U.S. up 24% from $4.2 billion to $5.2 billion.

Principal U.S. Officials

Ambassador--Francis J. Ricciardone, Jr.
Deputy Chief of Mission--Jess L. Baily

Counselors

Political Affairs--Yuri Kim
Political-Military Affairs--Edward G. Stafford
Economic Affairs--Laird Treiber
Regional Affairs--Thomas Sylvester
Consular Affairs--Laurence Tobey
Management Affairs--Richard Jaworski
Public Affairs--Mark Wentworth
Agricultural Affairs--Clay Hamilton
Commercial Affairs--Michael Lally
Senior Defense Official--Brig. Gen. James "Ed" Daniel

The U.S. Embassy:
110 Ataturk Boulevard
Kavaklidere, Ankara 06100
tel: (90) (312) 455-5555.

Chapter 2: Economy

Market Overview

Turkey's rapidly expanding economy, political and economic stability, and the possibility of EU membership has attracted the attention of a variety of American companies. In 2011, U.S. exports to Turkey reached a record $15 billion, a 34% increase from 2010. That trend is expected to continue, however an expected economic slowdown in Turkey in 2012 might give pause to some importers' buying decisions. Turkey's financial sector is stronger than that of many other countries, in part due to a series of reforms in the wake of the 2001 financial crisis, which left Turkish banks better leveraged than many of their U.S. and European counterparts. However, banks here remain hesitant to extend trade and project credit.

Across many sectors, U.S. exporters have excellent immediate and medium-term prospects in this diverse market. Perhaps the most important sector for the next decade will be energy. Electricity demand has been growing at 6.4 percent a year, and will continue to grow rapidly. Turkey realizes it must prepare for continued economic growth by adding now to its generating capacity to meet that demand. U.S. suppliers and service companies should look into energy sector as it relates to electricity and gas distribution, power generation and renewable energies, particularly wind and solar.

Opportunities exist in telecommunications services and equipment, safety and security equipment and services, automotive aftermarket, medical equipment, pharmaceuticals, R&D, transportation infrastructure and higher education services. Turkey sends the largest number of students among all European countries – around 12,000 each year – to U.S. colleges and universities. Turkish companies are eager partners for American firms, and seek technology and financing to grow their businesses.

In recent years, Turkey's market reforms, strong growth and economic and political stability have attracted Foreign Direct Investment (FDI). Despite a decline in FDI inflows as a result of the global economic crisis, cumulative FDI in Turkey now stands at $ 88 billion, with a 74% increase FDI in 2011. Cumulative American investment in Turkey is officially about $6-7 billion – a number which is understated because of U.S. company investments through third countries. In 2011, U.S. green field investments by Cummins, Pratt and Whitney, AES and Dow signaled increasing U.S. interest in Turkey. Turkey requires further investment; however excessive bureaucracy, an unpredictable legal system and weak intellectual property protection impedes further FDI growth. Market access issues in pharmaceuticals and genetically-modified agricultural products make these two sectors particularly difficult for American firms in Turkey.

In 2005, the EU and Turkey began formal EU accession negotiations. Turkey has adopted many European Union directives, regulations and laws in anticipation of accession. While continued delays have cooled popular interest in EU membership, Turkey's political and business leadership remains committed to joining the EU, and the current government understands that the process itself contributes to Turkey's global competitiveness.

Turkey is a long-term ally of the United States and a charter member of NATO with strong links to global institutions. Turkey has a key role to play in most of the major regional issues facing the United States. Our two countries currently enjoy a close and vibrant partnership, extending into key issues such as Syria, Iraq, Afghanistan and Cyprus. However, bilateral relations have been occasionally difficult. Under the Obama administration, continued high-level government contacts have created a constructive atmosphere, with a special emphasis on building bilateral commercial relations. The governments Framework for Strategic Economic and Commercial Cooperation and the private sector led U.S.-Turkish Business Council are examples of intensified efforts to increase bilateral trade and investment. Over 1,000 American firms are registered in Turkey, ranging from large multinationals to small and medium size firms. While Turkey's economic growth in 2012 is expected to slow, the longer-term prospects for many American firms in Turkey remain excellent.

Market Challenges

The Republic of Turkey is a complex and challenging market requiring adaptability and persistence.

U.S. exporters face many of the same challenges that exist in other semi-developed countries, such as contradictory policies, regulations and documentation requirements, lack of transparency in tenders and other procurement decisions, and a time consuming, unpredictable judiciary and legal and regulatory framework. Careful planning and patience are the keys to success in Turkey.

Market Opportunities

The Republic of Turkey's movement toward membership in the European Union is creating momentum to adopt European business regulations and standards in Turkey, thereby ultimately making it easier to sell and conduct business in this market. Similarly, reforms since 2001 have created a strong and stable economy that attracts foreign investment, which in turn will be followed by needed capital improvements and demand for new products and services.

The U.S Commercial Service in Turkey has identified a number of market opportunities, described below, for U.S. firms and continues to work with companies to enter the Turkish market, expand market share, or jointly enter third country markets.

Turkey is the commercial hub of the region, and U.S. companies should consider using Turkish partners to access business opportunities throughout Central Asia, the Caucasus, the Middle East and even Africa. Turkish partners know these neighboring markets well.

Market Entry Strategy

While there are many significant opportunities for U.S. companies in Turkey, there are also obstacles accessing them. Any market entry strategy for Turkey should begin with a thorough understanding of the costs and benefits in the market.

One of the most successful proven ways to access the market quickly is to work with an experienced local partner. This partner could be in the form of a local representative, liaison office, agent, distributor, stocking distributor, etc. The local partner brings knowledge of the local regulatory framework, language and contacts to the table. As the business develops, companies may open subsidiaries and make further local investments to expand their market share.

Economic Background

Nonagricultural economic activity is concentrated in four regions, centered, respectively, around the Sea of Marmara, Edirne on the west coast, the Adana–Mersin–İskenderun triangle along the Mediterranean Sea, and Ankara. In 2007 a large share of Turkey's major enterprises remained in state hands, including all of the transportation, utilities, and communications infrastructure, many basic industries, and about 30 percent of the assets in the banking sector. After failing to fulfill earlier privatization plans, in 2004 Turkey announced plans to privatize a wide range of industries, including tobacco and sugar processing, communications, and energy. Although no target dates were set, pressure from international financial institutions caused Turkey to begin privatization in most sectors by 2007.

Beginning in the 1980s, a number of cities in the Asian part of Turkey, known as the Anatolian Tigers, have shown particular economic growth in the private sector. The economy has been plagued by high inflation and high fiscal deficits. Those conditions improved somewhat beginning in 2004 as private investment increased significantly and the inflation rate declined.

The International Monetary Fund has exerted strong pressure and support for reform of the economic system.

In 2006 Turkey's state revenues totaled US$171.3 billion, and its expenditures totaled US$129.4 billion, creating a surplus of US$41.9 billion. In 2005 revenues were US$138 billion and expenditures, US$146.1 billion, resulting in a deficit of US$8.1 billion. In 2004 the deficit was US$30.3 billion. With assistance from International Monetary Fund programs, tax collection has become more efficient in the early 2000s, improving budget administration. Inflation has been a chronic problem in Turkey's economy. Between 1994 and 1999, the average yearly rate was 85 percent. However, in 2004 the rate dropped below 9 percent, the lowest since 1982, and it has remained at about that level since that time. The rate for 2007 was 8.5 percent.

Turkey is self-sufficient in most foods, although some agricultural commodities are imported. A relatively large percentage of Turkey's land is devoted to agriculture, but the productivity of agricultural lands varies greatly. The fields in western Turkey and along the southern coast are most productive, but physical conditions and greater transportation distances make agriculture substantially less profitable in other regions. The principal agricultural exports are cotton, fruits, hazelnuts, tobacco, and wheat. Other important agricultural products are barley, corn, oilseeds, olives, potatoes, sugar beets, and tea. The most important livestock are cattle, chickens, goats, and sheep, but livestock raising has declined significantly since the 1980s.

The efficiency of the agricultural sector is limited by the predominance of small, non-mechanized farms on which a disproportionately large segment of the population (27 percent in 2007) depends for its livelihood. Output varies substantially according to weather conditions. The Southeastern Anatolia Project, a federal program aimed at raising the development level of nine of Turkey's most impoverished provinces, has a substantial agricultural component. Among the project's goals is an extensive series of dams and canals in the Firat (Euphrates) Valley, scheduled for completion in 2010. The project will provide irrigation to improve agricultural productivity in the southeast. State support, an important component of agricultural enterprises, often has been poorly distributed and without proportionate returns. In the early 2000s, the government reduced agricultural support and began restructuring marketing systems.

In 2000 the extent of Turkey's forests was estimated at 10.2 million hectares. However, the forests of eastern Anatolia are not suitable for harvesting. The only usable timber comes from the Black Sea coastal region, and timber does not make a significant contribution to the economy. Because poor management and infrequent cutting have left many forests over- mature, only about 20 percent of the total forested area is classified as commercially exploitable.

In 2003 Turkey's timber industry produced a total of 16 million cubic meters of wood products, about 32 percent of which was fuelwood. Forest protection by the state is handicapped by the dependence of local populations on trees for fuel. In 2004 forestry contributed 0.4 percent of gross domestic product.

Despite Turkey's long coastline, fishing is not an important contributor to the economy. The fishing industry is concentrated on the coasts of the Black Sea and the Sea of Marmara, where output has been cut by pollution and over-fishing. In 2002 Turkey's fish catch totaled 567,000 tons, a substantial decrease from the annual totals of the 1990s. Anchovies accounted for more than 60 percent of the catch. A small aquaculture industry also exists. In 2004 fishing contributed 0.4 percent of gross domestic product.

Turkey's major mining operations, formerly controlled by state-owned companies, were increasingly privatized in the early 2000s. During that period, aluminum, chrome, copper, and silver mines moved into the private sector. Boron, of which Turkey has 60 percent of the world supply, is the most important non-fuel mineral. Its extraction remains a state monopoly. Based on new discoveries and foreign investment in the early 2000s, the output of gold and soda ash have increased significantly. Gold reserves are estimated at 450 tons. By far the most important mineral product is lignite coal, reserves of which were estimated at 10.6 billion tons in 2008. Turkey's low-quality lignite, burned mainly in power stations, is highly polluting. The output of hard coal has declined, reaching 3.3 million tons in 2002. Hard coal reserves are estimated at 1.2 billion tons. Marble is the most important mineral export.

Turkey's diverse manufacturing sector satisfies domestic demand for a wide variety of products; the main manufactured exports are consumer goods. Textiles and clothing account for 15 percent of all manufacturing and about one-third of manufactured exports. However, much of this production is unreported because it is in the "informal" sector. The most important textile product is cotton cloth. Besides textiles, the most important consumer items produced are televisions, automobiles, refrigerators, washing machines, and vacuum cleaners. The most important heavy industrial products are processed fuels, steel, cement, tractors, and fertilizers. Most manufacturing enterprises are privately owned, but the size of such enterprises varies greatly, and the state has influenced the relative growth of industries by providing disproportionate investment and incentives. Multinational companies are present in many light and heavy industries. Foreign auto companies—Fiat, Honda, Hyundai, Renault, and Toyota—have plants in Turkey. The industry produced nearly 1 million vehicles in 2006. Other industries such as appliances are mainly Turkish-owned. A large proportion of the appliances, consumer electronics, and vehicles manufactured in Turkey are exported. The largest privately owned industrial company is the Arcelik firm, which manufactures a wide variety of consumer products.

Traditionally, the construction industry has made an important contribution to the economy. However, construction's contribution declined in the late 1990s and early 2000s because of a reduction in demand for domestic and foreign building projects and because of Turkey's 2001 economic crisis. Expansion resumed at a moderate rate in 2004, and in 2005 and

2006 the growth rate was about 20 percent per year. In the early 2000s, the industry's foreign operations expanded, particularly in Russia, Turkmenistan, Kazakhstan, Saudi Arabia, and Afghanistan.

Coal is the only fossil fuel that Turkey possesses in abundance, meaning that large amounts of oil and natural gas are imported. In the early 2000s, the domestic distribution of fuels and electricity has been reformed to meet European Union standards. Distribution of natural gas, nearly all of which is imported, is to be privatized by 2009. Since the 1990s, Turkey has attempted to substitute cleaner natural gas for highly polluting domestic coal. In the early 2000s, about two-thirds of the 1.1 billion cubic feet of natural gas that Turkey imported was used by the electric power industry. Russia is the main supplier of natural gas; its share of Turkey's total imports is expected to rise from the 2003 figure of 25 percent to 58 percent in 2010. Other major suppliers are Iran and Azerbaijan. In 2005 Turkey's domestic oil output was about 45,000 barrels per day, about half the level of 1990, and it was forecast to fall by nearly 50 percent by 2011.

Turkey imports about 90 percent of its oil, mainly from Iran, Iraq, Russia, Saudi Arabia, and Syria. The demand for oil is expected to grow by about 20 percent from 2006 to 2011. Turkey's location along several international oil and gas pipelines eases transport. Ceyhan, on the Black Sea coast, is the terminus of the Baku–Tbilisi–Ceyhan oil pipeline, which was completed in 2006. Because the demand for electric power doubled in the 1990s, Turkey became a net importer of electricity, as domestic generating capacity was unable to keep up with demand.

Although in 2006 Turkey's generating capacity of 35,000 megawatts exceeded demand, plans called for increasing that amount to 67,000 megawatts by 2010 in anticipation of increased demand. In the early 2000s, domestic power supply was inefficient because new plants came online slowly, and industry privatization stalled. Occasional power outages have occurred, and electricity costs are among the highest in Europe. In 2008 a deal with Iran linked the two countries' electric systems, providing Turkey a backup supply when its grid fails. In 2007 TEAS, the state power generation and distribution company, still controlled 90 percent of the electric power market through its 15 thermoelectric and 30 hydroelectric plants. However, most of the plants in the next expansion phase are to be privately owned.

Since 2002 an independent Energy Market Regulatory Authority has overseen privatization and distribution. This agency is considered an important improvement in Turkey's energy management. Turkey abandoned plans for its first nuclear power plant in 2000 and again in 2005; in 2007 a controversial new plan called for a nuclear plant to open at Sinop in 2014. Turkey is considered to have substantial unused supplies of hydroelectric, wind, and solar power.

In the early 2000s, the contribution of service industries to the gross domestic product has increased (from 53 percent in 1998 to more than 60 percent in 2007), particularly in the areas of trade, catering, and personal services. Banking, the most important of Turkey's financial services, has undergone significant changes in the early 2000s. The current system is based on the Banks Act of 2005, which improved the inspection system, raised the standards for institutional participation in the industry, and simplified the process of bank mergers and takeovers. The financial crisis of 2001, for which the banks were partly responsible, had a severe impact on the sector. The resulting rationalization of the banking system reduced the number of banks by about one-third to 36, leaving the five largest banks with more than 50 percent of total assets. Those five private banks are part of large conglomerates with interests in many other sectors. Three state banks control about 30 percent of the industry's assets; their privatization has proceeded slowly.

Beginning in 2005, the participation of foreign banks had increased substantially. Since the 1990s, the Istanbul Stock Exchange has been quite active, although political developments have caused substantial volatility. Between 2004 and 2006, daily trading volume increased by 65 percent. In 2004 the exchange listed 291 companies, including some of the largest in Turkey. However, equity in many companies is unavailable for public trading. Most of Turkey's large insurance companies are connected with banks or international insurance firms. Per capita insurance expenditures, averaging US$80 per year in 2005, are the lowest in the industrialized world. Reform of the industry's regulatory structure, a requirement for membership in the European Union, has been proposed and tabled for several years. Until such reform, the National Treasury is the regulating agency. Small enterprises have dominated retail trade. However, in the early 2000s large Turkish chains such as Migros, Gima, and Tansas and foreign companies such as Metro of Germany, Carrefour of France, and Tesco of Britain occupied an expanding share of the retail sector. Shopping malls and supermarkets are increasingly common.

Turkey has taken advantage of its wide variety of scenic and historic locations, particularly along its southern and western coasts, to build a substantial tourism industry based on local ownership of hotels and restaurants. Some 19.8 million tourists visited Turkey in 2006, an increase of 90 percent over 2000. This activity generated revenues estimated at US$16.9 billion and provided an important source of foreign currency.

In 2007 Turkey's labor force was estimated at 23.5 million. However, a large part of this force (officially estimated at 11 million in 2004) works in the "informal sector," making measurement of its activities difficult. Another 3 million work in European Union and Middle Eastern countries. About 41 percent of the official workforce is occupied in services, 36 percent in agriculture, and 23 percent in construction and industry. In the early 2000s, the shift of labor away from agriculture and into services accounted for a significant increase in overall labor productivity. Industrial labor is heavily unionized, but the government has restricted some union activities. The largest unions are the Turkish Confederation of Labor and the Labor Unions Confederation. Total union membership is estimated at 3 million.

In early 2008, unemployment was estimated at 10.8 percent overall, compared with 10.4 percent in 2007. However, unemployment among the youngest age cohorts was estimated at nearly 20 percent. The overall rate was 12.7 percent in urban areas and 7.6 percent in rural areas. Another 4 percent of the workforce was considered underemployed. Although inflation has depressed wage values, in the early 2000s a series of sharp increases brought the 2008 minimum wage to US$483 per month. Wage disparities are great between eastern and western Turkey. Women account for only about one-quarter of the overall workforce but for 60 percent of the agricultural workforce. Remittances from Turks working abroad, chiefly in Germany and Saudi Arabia, have been an important source of national income. In the early 2000s, annual remittance figures have varied considerably, in part because of economic cycles in Turkey. The highest figure was US$5 billion in 1998.

Beginning in the late 1970s, Turkey has liberalized what was a policy of import substitution and protection of domestic industries by import restrictions. In the 1990s, export subsidies were abolished, and trade with the European Union (EU) increased slowly and steadily. Turkey was admitted to the World Trade Organization (WTO) in 1995. In 1996 a customs union was established between Turkey and the EU, abolishing tariffs on industrial products for both sides. The same relationship was established with all countries entering the EU after 1996, with the exception of Cyprus. An agreement on agricultural products retains tariffs on some agricultural imports from EU countries. In 1999 Turkey revised its customs legislation in accordance with EU standards. Between 1990 and 2007, the EU share of Turkey's exports remained steady between 51 and 56 percent, and the EU share of Turkey's imports also remained steady between 42 and 47 percent. Throughout that period, Germany remained among Turkey's primary trade partners, although that country's percentage of total trade (11.4 percent of exports and 10.6 percent of imports in 2006) diminished steadily in the early 2000s.

In the early 2000s, both export and import trade with the United States declined somewhat. In 2007 the United States accounted for 6 percent of Turkey's exports, compared with 7.7 percent in 2004, and for 4.5 percent of its imports, compared with 5 percent in 2004. In the early 2000s, a larger share of Turkey's imports came from the Commonwealth of Independent States (CIS), mainly because of reliance on natural gas from Russia, than had been the case during the 1990s. In 2007 Russia accounted for 12.8 percent of Turkey's imports (overtaking Germany as the largest import supplier), and the CIS as a whole accounted for 8.2 percent of Turkey's exports. Turkey also has bilateral trade relationships with the member nations of the European Free Trade Association (Iceland, Liechtenstein, Norway, and Switzerland), Albania, Bosnia and Herzegovina, Croatia, Egypt, Israel, Macedonia, Morocco, the Palestinian Territories, and Syria.

In the early 2000s, agricultural products dropped below 10 percent of Turkey's exports. Minerals and mineral products accounted for about 5 percent. In 2006 finished textiles accounted for about 23 percent. Other important exported manufactured products were steel, construction materials, appliances, televisions, and motor vehicles. Substantial unofficial trade occurs with neighboring countries of the Middle East and the CIS. The value of such trade in 2006 was estimated at US$6.4 billion. Fuels are the leading "official" imported commodity. Others are chemical products and machinery and transport equipment. Russia and Saudi Arabia are the chief suppliers of fuels. Other major suppliers of imports are the EU countries, Switzerland, Japan, and China. Between 2004 and 2006, imports from China more than doubled.

In 2007 Turkey's imports had a total value of US$156.9 billion, and its exports were valued at US$110.5 billion. Thus, the trade deficit for 2007 was US$46.4 billion, continuing a persistent trend. Between 2003 and 2006, the trade deficits were, respectively, US$21.8 billion, US$25 billion, US$28.7 billion, and US$35.7 billion.

In the early 2000s, Turkey's balance of payments has varied widely, although it was negative every year from 2000 through 2004. In 2007 the current account showed a deficit of US$38 billion, and the capital account showed a surplus of US$48.5 billion. The overall balance of payments for 2007 was US$12 billion. In 2007 Turkey's external debt totaled US$240 billion. When measured as a percentage of gross domestic product, this amount was a decrease of 7 percent compared with the average percentage (57 percent) for the years 2002–6.

Because of political uncertainty and the structure of Turkey's investment system, foreign direct investment (FDI) was relatively low in the first years of the 2000s, exceeding US$2 billion in only one year between 1999 and 2004. The total for 2004 was about US$2 billion, but legislative changes stimulated substantial increases beginning in 2005. Between 2005 and 2007, the total increased from US$8.7 billion to US$22 billion. FDI increases in 2006 were based particularly on activity in the banking and telecommunications sectors. In early 2008, foreign portfolio investment was estimated at about US$100 billion. A US$1.5 billion power plant near İskenderun, completed in 2004 by the STEAG utilities company of Germany, is the largest direct investment ever by a German company in Turkey.

Automotive companies in France, Italy, Japan, South Korea, and the United States participate in multinational partnerships with Turkey. In 2004 a Japanese consortium began building a railroad tunnel under the Bosporus, scheduled for completion in 2010. The United States–based General Dynamics Corporation has invested substantially in fighter aircraft manufacture in Turkey, and in the early 2000s Turkey's arms procurement policy encouraged joint projects and the licensing of production of foreign designs.

In January 2005, a currency reform established the new Turkish lira, which was worth 1 million of the previous unit, the Turkish lira. In August 2008, the exchange rate was about 1.2 new Turkish liras to the U.S. dollar. Thus, in 2008 the new lira was stronger against the dollar than the old lira had been in 2003, when the average rate was slightly more than 1.5 million to the dollar. Turkey's fiscal year is the calendar year.

Chapter 3: Market Features and Opportunities

Unique Geographic Location
Turkey is at the center of an economic and political area known as "Eurasia", where three regions of the world, Europe, the former Soviet Union and the Middle East intersect. The proximity to the Balkans and the rest of Europe as well as to the growing emerging markets in Central Asia, the Middle East and North Africa creates unique business opportunities. The experience of more than 7000 foreign capital establishments, including over 100 of the Fortune Top 500 companies, confirms Turkey as a predominant investment location and export platform. US companies like Coca-Cola, Procter & Gamble and Phillip Morris, as well as international investment institutions like the World Bank Group's International Finance Corporation already have selected Turkey as a regional base.

Turkey is the leading investor in Caucasian and Central Asian Turkic Republics. Due to her strong cultural and historic ties, Turkey provides privileged access and a perfect base to develop business with these countries.

The international image of Turkey in terms of a destination for investment is generally shaped by the diverse market opportunities, both domestic and export-oriented, that Turkey offers. The potential of these markets covers over 1 billion consumers, including:

High-income European markets (approx. 600 million), Emerging Russia, Caucasia and Central Asia markets (approx. 250 million),

Diverse and expanding Middle East and North Africa markets (approx. 160 million).

Huge and Growing Domestic Market
Turkey's population is approximately 67 million. Turkey is projected to continue to constitute one of the largest populations in the Middle East and Eastern Europe. The domestic market is predominantly urban, with at least 17 major cities having a population in excess of 1 million, led by Istanbul, Ankara and Izmir. The population is much younger than European countries, with over 60% of the population below the age of 35. The improving consumption patterns and purchasing power, with a growing middle class, are important features of the domestic market. The average annual GDP growth rate of 4.6 % over the 1995-2000 period, well above many other countries, implies a continuing robust growth potential. With Turkey's population growth rate having fallen from over 2% to roughly 1.5%, it is on the verge of entering a 'golden demographic period' similar to what East Asia experienced in the 1980s, where the productive working population is largest relative to children and retirees, providing the potential for even more rapid income growth.

Only a few emerging markets in the world have the potential of attracting investment both for export as well as for their domestic market. Turkey is in such a privileged position to create a 'virtuous investment cycle', with a more competitive domestic business environment further strengthening Turkey as a platform for exports, and exports in turn stimulating firms to upgrade and better serve the domestic market.

EU Customs Union and Accession Partnership

In 1996, a Customs Union between the European Union and Turkey came into effect, thereby creating the closest economic and political relationship between the EU and any non-member country. Essentially the Customs Union gives Turkey improved access to the group of countries previously known as the Common Market. It guarantees the free circulation of industrial goods and processed agricultural products. Customs duties and charges have been abolished and non-tariff barriers are prohibited. The Customs Union involves harmonization of Turkey's commercial and competition policies including intellectual property laws with those of the European Union and it extends most of the EU's trade and competition rules to the Turkish economy. The chief characteristic of the Customs Union is that goods move freely between the EU and Turkey without being subject to customs duties or quantitative restrictions; it covers all aspects of trade and commercial policy to ensure there is a "level playing field" for Turkish and European firms.

The Helsinki European Council in 1999 launched Turkey's formal EU accession process based on the same criteria as applied to all other candidate States. This has allowed Turkey to benefit from a pre-accession strategy to stimulate and support its increasing economic and political harmonization to EU standards. EU financial support for the continuing reforms contained in Turkey's National Program for the Adoption of the Acquis has been formalized in a 2001 Accession Partnership.

In late December 2004 the EU offered to begin membership talks with Turkey starting on October 3, 2005. EU leaders said the aim of the talks - which could take up to 15 years - would be full membership. As part of the agreement, Turkey agreed to extend an existing trade accord to the newest 10 E.U. members, which include Cyprus

Black Sea Economic Co-operation

Turkey is a leading party to the Black Sea Economic Co-operation (BSEC) Agreement, together with other regional countries. The BSEC Agreement highlights the need for adoption of a regional strategy for sustainable development – its objective is a free trade zone between the member states.

Established in 1992, the BSEC is composed of 11 countries: Albania, Armenia, Azerbaijan, Bulgaria, Georgia, Greece, Moldova, Romania, Russia, Turkey and Ukraine. Austria, Egypt, Israel, Italy, Poland, the Slovak Republic and Tunisia have been granted observer status. In 2001, BSEC countries had more than 5 percent of total world trade. More than 5 percent of the world's population lives in BSEC countries and the total BSEC area is around 20 million square kilometers. These figures indicate the importance of BSEC in the global economic order. It is expected that the significance of the BSEC region in economic and political terms will grow considerably over the coming years due to its geostrategic location, size and command over natural resources – particularly natural gas, oil and coal.

Openness to Global Trade and Investment

In addition to trade agreements with the EU and Black Sea countries, Turkey maintains an extremely liberal trade and investment regime with all countries, in conformity with its membership of international institutions such as the WTO,

MIGA and OECD. Turkey has signed additional Free Trade Agreements with EFTA, Hungary, Israel, Romania, Lithuania, Estonia, Czech Republic, Latvia, Slovakia, Slovenia, Bulgaria, Poland, Macedonia, Croatia and Bosnia-Herzegovina. Additional FTAs are being prepared with Albania, Morocco, Tunisia, Egypt, Palestine, Pakistan, South Africa, Mexico and Lebanon. Turkey has signed Bilateral Agreements on the Promotion and Protection of Investments with 67 countries, and is in negotiations with 9 additional countries. These agreements do not bring any new burdens to the concerned countries while providing additional economic and legal assurances to investors.

Energy Production and Transit Opportunities

Turkey has launched fundamental reform in its domestic electricity and natural gas sectors in 2001, leading to a liberal and transparent market model. Privatization and increased private sector participation is on the agenda for generation and distribution assets in electricity, and for distribution, trading (import and sales) and storage activities in the natural gas sector. Turkey's hydro generating capacity includes the huge integrated hydroelectric and irrigation South-East Anatolia Project (GAP), which among other objectives seeks to reduce Turkey's regional disparity in economic prosperity, employment and infrastructure. The new market model brings Turkey in line with the EU energy sector, with large eligible consumers free to select their own electricity and gas suppliers in 2003.

Turkey looks set to become a major energy transit country as well. With construction on the Baku-Tbilisi-Ceyhan crude oil pipeline begun in September 2002, Turkey seeks to bring new oil supplies to Western markets from the Caspian region, especially from Azerbaijan and Kazakhstan. Turkey also is diversifying its sources of natural gas through the construction of new gas pipelines from Azerbaijan, Turkmenistan and Iran, and a new route from Russia under the Black Sea (Blue Stream) has been completed. Turkey thereby prospectively offers an alternate path for gas from the Middle East and Central Asia into the major West European markets. In this context, feasibility studies to construct gas pipelines between Turkey and Greece to transmit gas via Greece and Italy within the context of the Southern Europe Gas Ring Project were finished in 2002. An Intergovernmental Agreement was signed between Turkey and Greece in February 2003 to implement the project and this was followed by a Natural Gas Sales and Purchase Agreement between Turkey and Greece in December 2003. Furthermore, BOTAS (Turkish Petroleum Pipeline Company) and an Italian natural gas company have launched studies to construct an offshore extension connecting Turkey, Greece and Italy. Studies also are underway for further large-scale electricity interconnectors to the UCTE network over Greece and the Balkans, to connect Turkey to the Western Europe Electricity System – in addition to the available power transmission links between Turkey and Bulgaria.

İSTAÇ Waste-to-Energy Power Plant:
USTDA is providing a $491,160 feasibility study grant in support of a municipal solid waste-to-energy (WTE) plant that would be implemented to provide a lasting solution to İSTAÇ's space limitation at the Odayeri Landfill site. The proposed WTE plant would have a 70 MW generation capacity, enough to

provide power to 350,000 households in the area, and would extend the remaining life of the landfill, reduce methane and odor emissions from the landfill site, and help İSTAÇ meet the municipal solid waste incineration targets.

Flood Forecasting and Early Warning System Feasibility Study
USTDA is funding a $507,420 feasibility study for the Turkish State Meteorological Service (TSMS) to develop an implementation plan to meet national-level Flood Forecasting and Early Warning System needs, including hardware, software, Geographic Information Systems (GIS), Relational Database Management Systems (RDMS), sensors, weather and water monitoring equipment, communications equipment, and modeling systems.

Emergency Management Sector Reverse Trade Mission:
USTDA funded a $226,466 reverse trade mission (RTM) to bring senior officials from the Prime Ministry Disaster and Emergency Management Authority and other Turkish agencies to the United States to meet with U.S. companies active in the emergency management sector and U.S. Government agencies. The RTM included visits to command and control centers, communications hubs, and emergency alert systems in the United States, and supports the Government of Turkey as it seeks to improve its emergency response capacity. The RTM took place in December 2010.

Chapter 4: Energy Efficiency Projects

The U.S. Department of Energy (DOE), in coordination with other U.S. agencies, is launching the Near-Zero Zone project, a demonstration project for industrial energy efficiency in Turkey. This interagency project, which has the support of the Turkish government and business organizations, will help industrial companies operating within the Izmir Ataturk Organized Industrial Zone (IAOSB) to reduce their energy intensity through a series of cost-effective efficiency upgrades. The project aims to demonstrate the impact that reducing energy consumption can have on companies' profitability, promote bilateral trade and investment, and serve as a replicable model for companies and industrial zones throughout Turkey.

Background

Turkey's economy is nearly twice as energy intensive as the OECD average and its industrial sector accounts for nearly 40 percent of its total energy consumption. The Near-Zero Zone project is meant to support Turkey's goals to reduce its industrial energy intensity while supporting Turkey's broader energy objectives, including reducing its reliance on energy imports, bolstering its energy security, and decreasing greenhouse gas emissions.

The IAOSB zone was selected to host the project for three primary reasons. First, with over 500 companies operating onsite, the zone provides opportunities to work with companies of varying sizes and diverse industries, enhancing the project's reach. Second, all of the zone's utilities – including electricity, heat, and wastewater treatment – are provided by the zone management company, further enhancing the energy efficiency opportunities in the zone. Finally, IAOSB is located near one of Turkey's largest ports and in a region with significant renewable energy potential, amplifying the potential for related bilateral trade and investment.

DOE will work with U.S. agencies including State, Commerce, Overseas Private Investment Corporation (OPIC), US Trade and Development Agency (TDA) and Export-Import Bank on this project. In addition to support from the U.S. and Turkish governments, additional participants may include European Bank for Reconstruction and Development (EBRD) and TURSEFF, an entity composed of four Turkish banks (Vakifbank, Akbank, Garanti Bank and Deniz Bank), as well as a number of private companies.

Key components of the Near-Zero Zone project will include:
Baseline Energy Audit: ORNL, a DOE national lab, is expected to conduct a preliminary energy audit for the participating companies. The audit will measure current energy usage and identify areas in which energy consumption can be reduced. This baseline data will ultimately be compared to data gathered at the project's conclusion to determine the impact of the energy efficiency measures.

Technical Assessments
For the IAOSB zone management company and approximately 20 participating companies, experts will develop detailed studies

of their energy consumption and issue recommendations on cost-effective energy efficiency measures. Each recommendation developed will include the cost of implementation and the potential impact on profitability so that companies can make business-motivated decisions. TDA and OPIC are expected to finance up to twenty technical assessments. Other financial sources may become available to fund additional technical assessments.

Energy Efficiency Upgrades

Based on the recommendations developed in the experts' technical assessments, the zone management and companies will be provided with information on appropriate equipment and service suppliers. The U.S. Commerce Department will provide direct access to a number of equipment and service suppliers through a trade delegation scheduled for autumn 2011. Companies will also be introduced to various lenders – including EBRD, TURSEFF, OPIC, Ex-Im and others – and offered financing options from which they can choose based on their business needs.

Results

After the IAOSB management company and other participating companies implement the energy efficiency measures they feel will enhance their productivity and profitability, an assessment of the project's impact on energy consumption will be completed. DOE has requested that Turkish business organizations disseminate the findings to their member companies through whatever means they believe will have the greatest impact. This is intended to make companies across Turkey aware of the positive effect that energy efficiency can have on their bottom line.

The project is intended to promote the adoption of similar energy efficiency measures by companies and industrial zones elsewhere in Turkey. Given the strong presence of Turkish firms in Central Asia, the Middle East and Europe, this project may also help create opportunities for industrial energy efficiency in those regions.

This pilot project represents a 'win-win' for Turkish and American companies, as well as the U.S. and Turkish governments. On the Turkish side, companies would benefit directly from U.S. technologies, financing, and associated reductions in energy costs while the government would benefit from the sharing of best practices and reduction in industrial sector energy consumption. On the U.S. side, companies would be able to provide equipment and services to up to 500 companies in the industrial zone, as well as to establish a strong foothold in Turkey's growing energy efficiency and clean energy markets. Meanwhile, the USG would make significant progress in advancing President Obama and Prime Minister Erdogan's shared commitment to increase bilateral trade and investment.

Project Timeline

Winter 2011: Conduct initial energy audit

Spring/Summer 2011: Prepare technical studies and issue recommendations

Fall 2011: Present companies in the zone with equipment/service and financing options

Winter/Spring/Summer 2012: Implement efficiency upgrades

Fall 2012: Complete final assessment and disseminate project results

Chapter 5: Business Organizations

Turkish World Business Council

Founding year: 2008

General Information

Founded with the decision taken by DEİK (Dış Ekonomik İlişkiler Kurulu - Foreign Economic Relations Board) on 26.12.2007 and by TOBB on 24.01.2008, as a part of DEİK; DTİK (Dünya Türk İş Konseyi - World Turkish Business Council) aims to gather all the small dispersed networks of Turkish entrepreneurs and successful Turkish professionals, who have gained authority in decision-making processes of big international companies abroad, under one big structure to waken and enhance the lobbying activities.

The president of the DTİK is Mr. M. Rifat Hisarcıklıoğlu and the president of the High Advisory Board of DTİK is Mr. Muhtar Kent (Chairman of the Coca Cola Company). DTİK is the only business council with a special purpose, a structure where there is no place for political concerns but a common goal for all: bringing together the whole Turkish business community, business associations, foundations and other similar Turkish organizations from 5 continents under the same roof.

The main goal of "World Turkish Business Council" (DTİK) is to boost the commercial and economical relations among the Turkish business community settled outside Turkey, to strengthen and disseminate the Turkish diaspora further, to create one main center for all kinds of problems that the Turkish entrepreneurs face abroad, and to lead the bids to establish a stronger image for Turkey in the World.

The Structure

President of TOBB / DEİK and DTİK Mr. M. Rifat HİSARCIKLIOĞLU

President of the Executive Board of DEİK Mr. Rona YIRCALI

President of the High Advisory Board of DTİK Mr. Muhtar KENT

Executive Board:

1- M.RİFAT HİSARCIKLIOĞLU- President of TOBB/DEİK

2- RONA YIRCALI- Member Chairman of DEİK Executive Board; Chairman of World Chambers Federation (WCF)

3- MUHTAR KENT- Member President of DTİK High Advisory Board Chairman of the Coca-Cola Company

4- RAHMİ KOÇ- Member Honorary Chairman of Koç Holding

5- GÜLER SABANCI-Member Chairman of the Sabancı Holding

6- ZEYNEL ABİDİN ERDEM- Member Member of Board of Directors of DEİK Chairman of DEİK Turkish-Spanish Business Council Chairman of Erdem Holding.

7- CAN AKIN ÇAĞLAR- Member General Manager of the Ziraat Bank

8- AHMET ÇALIK-Member Chairman of the Çalık Holding

9- ZEKİ PİLGE- Member President of Region Commitee of Eurasia

10- NEDİM DÜZENLİ-Member President of Region Commitee of America

11- TUNÇ ÖZKAN- Member President of Region Commitee of Africa, Middle East and the Gulf

12- NEJDET DEMİRYÜREK- Member President of Region Commitee of Asia – Pacific

13- TURGUT TORUNOĞULLARI- Member President of Region Commitee of Europe

14- ÖMER SÜSLİ- Member Member – Region Commitee of Europe

15-OSMAN ŞAHBAZ- Member Member – Region Commitee of Europe

High Advisory Board:

1- MUHTAR KENT-President Chairman of Coca Cola Company

2- ATİLLA DOĞUDAN- Member President of the DO&CO Administrative Board

3- VURAL ÖGER-Member Chairman of ÖGER Group and ÖGER Holding

4- NİHAT SORGEÇ- Member Chairman of BWK

5- MÜBARİZ MANSİMOV- Member PALMALİ Holding- President of the Administrative Board

6- ATIL KUTOĞLU- Member Fashion Designer

7- ASLI F. BAŞGÖZ- Member White&Case Vice President

Turkish- American Business Council

Founding year: 1985

Aim

The primary objective of the Business Council (TAIK) is to contribute to efforts to improve the environment for bilateral trade and industrial cooperation. It provides a forum for deliberations on new avenues and forms of bilateral trade and on policy recommendations for the removal of tariff and non-tariff barriers to trade.

Identification

Counterpart Organization: American-Turkish Council (ATC) Chairman of Turkish Chapter: Haluk Dinçer Company and Position: H.Ö. Sabancı Holding A.Ş., President of the Retail GroupChairman of Counterpart Chapter: Ambassador Richard L. Armitage Company and Position: United States Former Deputy Secretary of State TAIK was formed in 1985 as the first business council in Turkey with the aim to enhance trade and investment relations between Turkey and the U.S.

Vision & Mission

TAIK' s vision is primarily to increase the volume of Turkey-US trade (as a minimum to Turkey-EU level), to be recognized as the source of information and networking on bilateral issues for both Turkish and US companies and to assist US companies to view Turkey as a key partner and destination for direct investments in the region.

TAIK subsequently operates with a mission to create platforms to facilitate the development of commercial and trade relations through its range of activities. With its broad range of activities that it undertakes and its wide-ranging international links, TAIK has set precedent to other organizations, in pursuit of similar goals.

Its Executive Committee is represented by the top-level executives of the leading companies in Turkey. Since its establishment, prominent names such as Ersin Faralyalı, Sedat Aloglu, Mustafa Koc, Akin Ongor, Dr. Vural Akisik and Dr. Yilmaz Arguden have chaired the Business Council.

Hostory

In 1986 nine principal private sector institutions in Turkey came together to create The Foreign Economic Relations Board, a non-profit, private sector organization which would strive to improve Turkey's economic relations internationally. As a result of the restructuring process in year 2006, DEİK's founding member institutions have increased to twenty-seven, whose broad base constituencies enable DEIK to represent Turkish corporations in virtually all sectors.

DEIK operates as an umbrella organization comprised of seventy-five Bilateral Business Councils. These Bilateral Business Councils are established by the interested Turkish companies and their foreign counterparts for the purpose of promoting business relations more effectively. Having a structured bilateral business council ensures an effective follow-up mechanism and enables the continuous flow of information to member companies on trade and industrial cooperation possibilities. TAIK, the largest, the oldest and most established Business Council, operates under the permanent secretariat of DEIK.

Since its foundation, the Council has benefited from the active support and encouragement of both the Turkish and U.S governments, and is privileged to host high ranking dignitaries. TAIK has a strategic relationship with various Business Development Organizations in the United States for the coordination of events to promote bilateral trade.

Committees

TAIK plans its activities through strategy and communications committees and industry-specific committees, namely construction, energy, IT, banking and finance, finance (non-banking), EU, education, health, automotive, telecommunications, textile, media, tourism, culture and arts, jewelry, defense, agri-business, retail, third countries and governmental affairs.

Annual Conference

The 'Joint Annual Conference' organized by TAIK and American Turkish Council every spring in Washington DC, creates further opportunities for member companies to exchange views on economic and political issues put forward by experts. The Conference attracts hundreds of business people as well as high-level government representatives from both countries addressing the key issues in different sectors. Panel discussions on issues such as 'trade and investment issues', 'banking and finance', 'agribusiness', 'energy', 'construction', 'foreign affairs and 'defense' are the usual highlights.

While in Washington, D.C, TAIK board members visit members of Congress, the Administration, think tanks, financial agencies and U.S. media representatives in order to exchange views on bilateral relations and to discuss policy recommendations for the removal of tariff and non-tariff barriers to trade and investment.

Exploring Business Prospects

TAIK exerts emphasis to cooperation in third countries and therefore has taken a proactive role in contributing to the processes of restructuring and rebuilding Iraq and Afghanistan as well as having undertaken various missions jointly with the Turkish – Eurasian Business Councils to the Republics of Central Asia, Ukraine and the Russian Federation, which yielded constructive results. Also, TAİK organized a seminar titled "Investment and Partnership Opportunities: Greece – Turkey – U.S." in collaboration with the Turkish-Greek Business Council, in 2006, New York. Such missions demonstrate the eagerness of Turkish companies to explore joint venture possibilities with companies in emerging and developing markets.

The Council benefits from the synergy that is generated by the environment which the DEIK network of seventy-five bilateral councils as well as the Black Sea Economic Cooperation creates. The Black Sea Economic Cooperation Business Council, which brings together the business communities of the twelve participating countries consisting of Albania, Armenia, Azerbaijan, Bulgaria, Georgia, Greece, Moldova, Romania, Russian Federation, Turkey, Serbia and Ukraine is represented by DEIK in Turkey.

Other Services and Activities
• employs a consultant in Washington, D.C. to maintain contacts pertaining to its business and lobbying activities as well as identify new business opportunities.

• organizes business seminars in different cities throughout the United States with local business organizations in order to develop opportunities for collaboration in business and investment areas. In this framework, seminars have been held in New York, Chicago, Orlando, Houston, Columbus, San Francisco, Boston, New Orleans, Los Angeles, Atlanta, Charlotte, Manchester, Shepherdstown and Pittsburgh.

• hosts briefing seminars with luncheons, dinners or receptions with its members for delegations of American businessmen, Congressmen, staffers visiting every year. During their visits, TAİK also organizes exclusive meetings with high-level government officials, business people and NGOs. Among the dignitaries whom TAİK hosted, US President Bill Clinton (1999), Hillary Clinton (1996), Dennis Hastert, the Speaker of the House of Representatives (2002), J. Donohue, the US Chamber of Commerce President (2002), W. Daley (1998) and Mosbacher (1991), US Secretaries of Commerce, Spencer Abraham (2004), US Secretary of Energy, Mineta (2004), US Secretary of Transportation, could be named. TAIK also hosts delegations of National War College, National Defense University, US-Asia Foundation, Foreign Policy Association, Georgetown University, Emory University, ACYPL during their Turkey visits.

• conveys the views of the Business Council at official platforms like the "Economic Partnership Commission" (EOK), Trade Investment Framework Agreement" (TIFA) meetings, in addition to occasions like the Prime Ministry and Ministry visits.

• organizes meetings to build domestic interest level in doing business with the U.S and educate the public on various aspects of the relations between the U.S. and Turkey. (For example, as part of the commemoration activities of TAIK's 20th Year Anniversary, a chain of "Anatolian-US Bridge" meetings have been organized in economically emerging cities in Turkey to inform the local businessmen about the economic potential and ways of doing business in the U.S.)

• conducts research on various dimensions of bilateral economic and business development, forwards comprehensive information to its members acquired via contacts / projects held in cooperation with government institutions, academic institutions, think tanks, international finance and other intermediary business institutions, both in Turkey and the US.

Chapter 6: Business Service Providers

Accounting, Auditing, and Tax Services

Ayhan Consulting
Contact: Can Ayhan, Certified Public Accountant & Financial Consultant
Aziziye Mh. Kirkpinar Sokak No:24-7 Cankaya
Ankara Turkey
Phone: +903124426489
Fax: +903124426499
Email: can@ayhanconsulting.com
Web: http://www.ayhanconsulting.com

Ayhan Consulting was established in 2009 by Mr. Can Ayhan, Certified Public Accountant in order to meet the requirements of the foreign and multinational companies operating in Turkey. Main services are; statory accounting outsourcing, tax and social security advisory, management reporting, budgeting and company establishment services. Main experienced sectors are; service, telecommunications, IT, defense, health, education and construction.

Isik Yeminli Mali Musavirlik A.S
Contact: Hakan Sahin, Partner
Beylerbeyi Burhaniye Mah. Attilla Sokak No:12 Uskudar
Istanbul Turkey
Phone: +902164225252
Fax: +902164225264

Email: hsahin@isik-ymm.com.tr
Web: http://www.isik-ymm.com.tr
BKR International is an association of independent auditing accounting and business advisory firms. BKR International represents the combined expertise of more than 140 member firms with 340 offices in over 70 countries around the world. Isik Yeminli Mali Musavirlik was established in 1990 by 5 certified public accountants who were former tax inspectors of the Ministry ofFinance and the former executives of the state organizations and major companies of the private sector. Today our firm turned out to be one of the leading independent audit firms in Turkey. Being an independent member of BKR International enables us to provide worldwide business services. To ensure the highest level of performance, we ensure an ongoing assessment of professional services. Isik Yeminli Mali Musavirlik A.S. is actively operating and providing its services under Tax Department, Audit Department, Consultancy Department, Outsource Services.

MK Strategic Consultancy Services Inc.
Contact: Selim Akalan, CPA
Eskisehir Yolu 9km. No:262 Tepe Prime A Blok Kat:14 No:83
Cankaya- Ankara Turkey
Phone: +90-312-473-3290
Fax: +90-312-473-3293
Email: info@mkmusavirlik.com
Web: http://www.mkmusavirlik.com
MK Consulting offers services in the areas of tax, accounting, audit, corporate finance, law, training and management. MK

Consulting produces strategy oriented professional solutions to sustain their clients' success.

Ozbek CPA

Contact: Sema Ozbek, CPA

Gulbahar Mah. Oya Apt. No:10-2

Mecidiyekoy-Sisli

Istanbul Turkey

Phone: +90-212-356-8000

Fax: +90-212-266-6767

Email: sema@ozbekcpa.com

Web: http://www.ozbekcpa.com

Our company provides service to the foreign companies who intend to our clients. Privacy, legislation, quality and deadlines are priority for OZBEKCPA.

Banking and Financial Services

EDS Consulting

Contact: Can Acarlar, President

Tunus Cad. Tunus Apt. 88-7 Kavaklidere-Ankara

Acarkent 10. Cad 55.Sok B816 Beykoz-Istanbul

Ankara-Istanbul Turkey

Phone: +905324511585

Fax: +903124688128

Email: can.acarlar@edsdevelopment.com

Web: http://www.edsdevelopment.com

EDS provide consultancy services to our clients mainly emphasis on power, energy, oil, gas, healthcare, real estate project developments. Companies also turn to EDS for assistance in large complex sales situations for sales strategy, commercial terms and conditions structuring, a transaction management. EDS is known for detailed research, extensive local contacts and indepth understanding of local requirements.

Building and Construction Services

Merc Global Group
Contact: M.Ali Merc, Managing Director
Fevzi Cakmak Sokak. No:30/15 Kizilay-Ankara Turkey
Phone: +903122303182
Fax: +903122303185
Email: mercglobal@biri.com.tr
Web: http://www.mercglobal.com.tr

Oil & Gas & Energy field & Site Support. Turkish manpower staffing & supplying. Project management and consulting engineering. Renewable Energy investment consulting. Real Estate project development and land searching foreign companies representing and consulting. Global manpower staffing & supplying. Oil & Gas Hr Training and certification. Preparing work & resident permits for foreigners pay rolling and office services for foreigners pay rolling and office services for foreigners camp preparing & management and catering.

Business Management Services

CS Business Management and Support Services
Contact: Cagatay Altunsoy, General Manager
Egs Business Park Zemin Kat No:70

Bakirkoy
Istanbul Turkey
Phone: +902124652215
Fax: +902124652216
Email: info@csy.com.tr
Web: http://csy.com.tr

CS is a consulting and business services company providing international business consulting, start-up, market and product launch, international sales, marketing and instant office services in Turkey.

Due to our extensive business experiences in Turkey and because of our background with diverse industries, our extensive relationships in politics and business, we are the professional partner for a successful Turkish market entry. In order to offer our customers compherensive services through synergy effects and to provide exceptional results, CS also formed strong partnerships with other professional service providers.

Due to this Synergy Alliance Partner Program our clients additionaly benefit from our exceptional combination of expertise, international experience and business connections, high level connections, high level connections through the effective use of global networks and the synergy of strong partnerships.

We would like to invite you as our client and partner to break new ground in Turkey by taking advantage of our years of experience, economic and political networks and effective partner strategies.

Merc Global Group

Contact: M.Ali Merc, Managing Director

Fevzi Cakmak Sokak. No:30/15 Kizilay-Ankara Turkey

Phone: +903122303182

Fax: +903122303185

Email: mercglobal@biri.com.tr

Web: http://www.mercglobal.com.tr

Oil & Gas & Energy field & Site Support. Turkish manpower staffing & supplying. Project management and consulting engineering. Renewable Energy investment consulting. Real Estate project development and land searching foreign companies representing and consulting. Global manpower staffing & supplying. Oil & Gas Hr Training and certification. Preparing work & resident permits for foreigners pay rolling and office services for foreigners pay rolling and office services for foreigners camp preparing & management and catering.

Business Associations

Merc Global Group

Contact: M.Ali Merc, Managing Director

Fevzi Cakmak Sokak. No:30/15 Kizilay-Ankara Turkey

Phone: +903122303182

Fax: +903122303185

Email: mercglobal@biri.com.tr

Web: http://www.mercglobal.com.tr

Oil & Gas & Energy field & Site Support. Turkish manpower staffing & supplying. Project management and consulting engineering. Renewable Energy investment consulting. Real Estate project development and land searching foreign companies representing and consulting. Global manpower staffing & supplying. Oil & Gas Hr Training and certification. Preparing work & resident permits for foreigners pay rolling and office services for foreigners pay rolling and office services for foreigners camp preparing & management and catering.

Business Consulting

APCO Worldwide
Contact: Zeynep Dereli, Managing Director
Muallim Naci Cad. 93-95 B Block Floor: 2
Kurucesme-Istanbul
Phone: +902122631003
Fax: +902122653338
Email: zdereli@apcoworldwide.com
Web: http://www.apcoworldwide.com

APCO Worldwide in Turkey provides clients with a full-service, integrated approach to communication, stakeholder engagement and business strategy. Clients count on us for a 360° perspective on stakeholder engagement, fresh thinking, deep insights, creative solutions and flawless execution that deliver lasting impact. With our office located in Istanbul and additional consultants in Ankara, APCO in Turkey draws on its experienced team locally and internationally to provide expert counsel to clients

ATS-Alternative Trade Strategies Consultancy Ltd.
Contact: Tolga Gonenli, Managing Partner
Sezai Selek Sokak No:8, Sart Apt. D:1, Nisantasi, 34365, Istanbul, Turkey
Phone: +90-212-219-1636
Fax: +90-212-219-1633
Email: tolga.gonenli@ats-consultancy.com

Alternative Trade Strategies (ATS) Consultancy is an international consultancy company specializing in market access, business development, regional partnerships, commercial and governmental networks, regional trade strategies.

ATS is also involved in representing qualified firms in the region as well as organizing industry specific trade events, specializing in defense, aerospace, security and ICT sectors such as the EMEA Intelligence trade event in Istanbul.

ATS serves their clients by implementing the use of experienced industry advisors, an in-house creative marketing agency and by implementing innovative and alternative ideas and technologies to constantly keep their clients one step ahead in the world of business. ATS promises, above all else, an understanding of strong business ethics, in compliance with the FCPA to support sustainable solutions towards the needs of their client's success.

CS Business Management and Support Services
Contact: Cagatay Altunsoy, General Manager
Egs Business Park Zemin Kat No:70
Bakirkoy
Istanbul Turkey

Phone: +902124652215
Fax: +902124652216
Email: info@csy.com.tr
Web: http://csy.com.tr

CS is a consulting and business services company providing international business consulting, start-up, market and product launch, international sales, marketing and instant office services in Turkey.

Due to our extensive business experiences in Turkey and because of our background with diverse industries, our extensive relationships in politics and business, we are the professional partner for a successful Turkish market entry. In order to offer our customers compherensive services through synergy effects and to provide exceptional results, CS also formed strong partnerships with other professional service providers.

Due to this Synergy Alliance Partner Program our clients additionaly benefit from our exceptional combination of expertise, international experience and business connections, high level connections, high level connections through the effective use of global networks and the synergy of strong partnerships.

We would like to invite you as our client and partner to break new ground in Turkey by taking advantage of our years of experience, economic and political networks and effective partner strategies.

Crossborder Corporate Consultancy Ltd.

Contact: Cigdem Bicik, Managing Partner

Buyukdere Cad.185 Kanyon Ofis

K.6 Levent

Istanbul Turkey

Phone: +90-212-319-7716/+90532-324-0085

Fax: +90-212-319-7600

Email: cigdemb@crossborder-cc.com

Web: http://www.crossborder-cc.com

Crossborder, established in 2006, is a boutique consultancy company based in Istanbul. Crossborder's experienced consultants provide high quality value added Corporate Finance and Management Consultancy services to local and international clients. Main areas of expertise include Crossborder M&A's, Private Equity and Project Financing. Crossborder advises clients in order to access all types of corporate finance resources, be it for the equity or debt needs of companies. Crossborder is the executive member of M&A Europe for Turkey. M&A Europe is a network of M&A boutiques network with members in more than 30 countries worldwide.

E-Consultancy

Contact: Huseyin Erim, Chairman

Hosderec Caddesi Halit Ziya Sokak 26-8

Cankaya

Ankara, 06540 Turkey

Phone: +90-532-258-0818

Fax: +90-312-442-6194

Email: huseyinerim@superonline.com; huseyinerim@e-consultancy.net

Web: http://www.e-consultancy.net

E-Consultancy is established in 2001 as a business provider, investor, partner and project management. Our main subjects are Energy (waste energy and renewable energy), Medical, Defense and Education & Training, Software * Electronics. From Istanbul Company (A&B Ltd). We distribute world famouse organic cosmetics. In the energy field we are cooperating with Alter Energy Canada and we planned to build some power stations some of Turkish cities using municipal waste. We have partner companies in Washington D.C, Florida and Cleveland. You may see the details in our web page. (www.e-consultancy.net). We have a good connections Middle East Countries, Eastern Europe, Ukraine, Africa and Caucasus Countries.

EDS Consulting

Contact: Can Acarlar, President

Tunus Cad. Tunus Apt. 88-7 Kavaklidere-Ankara

Acarkent 10. Cad 55.Sok B816 Beykoz-Istanbul

Ankara-Istanbul Turkey

Phone: +905324511585

Fax: +903124688128

Email: can.acarlar@edsdevelopment.com

Web: http://www.edsdevelopment.com

EDS provide consultancy services to our clients mainly emphasis on power, energy, oil, gas, healthcare, real estate project developments. Companies also turn to EDS for assistance in large complex sales situations for sales strategy, commercial terms and conditions structuring, a transaction management.

EDS is known for detailed research, extensive local contacts and indepth understanding of local requirements.

Fara Group Inc.
Contact: Allen Collinsworth, Managing Director
Akatlar-Istanbul
Phone: 5337760256
Email: acollinsworth@faragroup.net
We are a frontier management organization with on the ground capacities in Turkey, Kazakhstan, and Iraq. Through reliable local partners, matched with our international standard of professionalism, we deliver efficiency and predictability to clients. Our specializations include both research (feasibility reports, market intelligence, background checks and expert sourcing) and operations management (quick service restaurants, real estate acquisition, and construction project management).

Foreign Market Consulting Ltd. Sti
Contact: Ozlem Ilica, Sales Manager
Sumer Korusu Evleri Kasimpati sokak No:25 Tarabya
Istanbul, 34457
Phone: +902123638055
Email: o.ilica@fmconsulting.info
Web: http://www.fmconsulting.info
FMConsulting, established in 1999, is an international consulting and service company located in Istanbul, specializing in strengthening the market position of our international clients in Turkey.We provide tailored research and consulting services based on your actual requirements, to give you an unparalleled service. Our locality, our experience and our proffesional know-

how ensure your satisfaction. With over 10 years experience and 300+ clients, we believe that long term partnerships are the most successful means of entering the Turkish market. For company formations, market research, business partner searches, finding customers and business administration services in Turkey and beyond, FMConsulting should be your first choice local partner.

Inspark Akilli Is Cozumleri
Contact: Serdar Susuz, General Manager
Arpaci Ali Sokak No: 8
Yenikoy
Istanbul Turkey
Phone: +902122998980
Fax: +902122990802
Email: info@inspark.com
Web: http://www.inspark.com

INSPARK Intelligent Business Solutions is an independent firm of consultants founded in 1990 and operating from Istanbul providing services throughout Europe. The company combines knowledge, excellence and a strong belief in providing a service suitable to customer budget. INSPARK has been created to be a leader in business and software consultancy, offering the highest value and knowledge in selection, implementation, development and support of business software. Our partners include strong US companies like Salesforce.com, Infor, Informatica, Successfactors, Box and Google. There are over 400 companies in Turkey that use our solutions like Coca Cola, Liberty Insurance, Abbott Pharmaceuticals, DHL Express, Shell Gas, WWF, Turkcell Global Bilgi, Sony.

Merc Global Group

Contact: M.Ali Merc, Managing Director
Fevzi Cakmak Sokak. No:30/15 Kizilay-Ankara Turkey
Phone: +903122303182
Fax: +903122303185
Email: mercglobal@biri.com.tr
Web: http://www.mercglobal.com.tr

Oil & Gas & Energy field & Site Support. Turkish manpower staffing & supplying. Project management and consulting engineering. Renewable Energy investment consulting. Real Estate project development and land searching foreign companies representing and consulting. Global manpower staffing & supplying. Oil & Gas Hr Training and certification. Preparing work & resident permits for foreigners pay rolling and office services for foreigners pay rolling and office services for foreigners camp preparing & management and catering.

The Istanbul Consulting Company

Contact: Turgut Ziyal, Managing Partner
Zekeriyakoy Visne 2 Bolgesi Gurgen S.3
Sariyer-Istanbul Turkey
Phone: +90-212-202-7434/+90-532-264-8911
Fax: +90-212-202-7433
Email: turgut.ziyal@theistanbulconsulting.com
Web: http://www.theistanbulconsulting.com

The Istanbul Consulting Company (TICC) has been established by Mr. Turgut Ziyal and Mr. Guldenir Kurtar in January 2011. Currently the team consists of six senior executives from banking and business environment of Turkey. TICC has experienced solution partners in legal counseling, taxation, auditing and incentive assistance. TICC provides full service support for foreign investors in Turkey. With its experienced team TICC offers fast solutions for companies planning to enter in Turkish market or to those already present in Turkey.

Car Services and Rentals

BTO Bilimtur Corp
Contact: Osman Imamoglu, Manager
Uskup Cad. 3A Cevre Sok Farabi
Ankara Turkey
Phone: +90-312-4687580
Fax: +90-312-468-7624
Email: oimamoglu@btobilimtur.com
Web: http://btobilimtur.com
Founded in 1995 . BTO offers airport transfers , daily rentals (with and without a driver) in Ankara and İstanbul. All our drivers have certificates in defensive driving ,first aid, anti-skid, and off –road driving. BTO annually perforrms over 7500 transfers.

Merc Global Group
Contact: M.Ali Merc, Managing Director
Fevzi Cakmak Sokak. No:30/15 Kizilay-Ankara Turkey
Phone: +903122303182
Fax: +903122303185
Email: mercglobal@biri.com.tr
Web: http://www.mercglobal.com.tr
Oil & Gas & Energy field & Site Support. Turkish manpower staffing & supplying. Project management and consulting

engineering. Renewable Energy investment consulting. Real Estate project development and land searching foreign companies representing and consulting. Global manpower staffing & supplying. Oil & Gas Hr Training and certification. Preparing work & resident permits for foreigners pay rolling and office services for foreigners pay rolling and office services for foreigners camp preparing & management and catering.

Customs Brokerage

Bilin Gumruk Musavirligi Ltd. Sti.
Contact: Saruhan Sarman, General Manager
Kaptanpasa Mah. Darulaceze Cad. Famas Is Merkezi
No:47 Kat: 8 Okmeydani-Sisli
Istanbul Turkey
Phone: +90-212-444-9-256
Fax: +90-212-222-0534
Email: saruhan@bilingumruk.com
Web: http://www.bilingumruk.com

Bilin Customs Brokeage was established at 1948 and of the leader in customs sector. It's our honour to publish that Bilin Customs Brokeage is serving 63.986(2011) declarations per a year. We manage around 88 business partners operation fastly, efficiency and with success by our 133 educated, experienced staff and professional management team. With our clean history, from the beginning we serve clean business to the business to the partners always by following ethics values. As we are customs solution partner of biggest companies in the world and Turkey.(e.g: GE, Nokia, Siemens Network, THY, THY Technic, Pratt & Whitney, Goodrich, Halliburton, Ceva Turkey and etc.)

we always follow our business with highest care and professional attitude. Our operation volume and customer satisfaction level which we touch at this moment is presented our achievement.

Debt Collection
TBS Turam & Donmez Avukatlik Ortakligi/TBS International Consulting Ltd.

Contact: C.Kemal Turam, Attorney at Law
Abide- Hurriyet Cad. Yonca Apt. No:148 Kat:5
Sisli,Istanbul Turkey
Phone: +902122316782
Fax: +902122190367
Email: kemal.turam@tbsavukatlar.com; zeynep.kaptan@tbsdanismanlik.com.tr
Web: http:///www.tbsavukatlar.com;http://www.tbsdanismanlik.com.tr

TBS works extensively on dept recovery and related litigation. Founded in 1989 by Cumhur Kemal Turam, TBS Lawyers, as of January 1st, 2010 continues to serve its clients as TBS Turam & Donmez Law Firm. Today, with a total staff of 125, TBS specializes in commercial litigation, bankruptcy and detailed legal consultancy to many local and international clients.

TBS International Consulting is a reflector of the professional work that TBS Turam & Donmez Law Firm has been doing over the last 24 years, but it was established as a seperate entity that delivers the same quality of service in investment consulting at very competitive rates in a one-stop-shop approach. TBS-IC's mission is to make its clients feel at home even when they are doing business. It's services vary from strategic partnership research (matchmaking) to debt collection.

Contact: Zeynep Kaptan, General Manager

Mobile: +90 549 627 9774

Education and Training Services

Foreign Market Consulting Ltd. Sti
Contact: Ozlem Ilica, Sales Manager
Sumer Korusu Evleri Kasimpati sokak No:25 Tarabya
Istanbul, 34457
Phone: +902123638055
Email: o.ilica@fmconsulting.info
Web: http://www.fmconsulting.info

FMConsulting, established in 1999, is an international consulting and service company located in Istanbul, specializing in strengthening the market position of our international clients in Turkey.We provide tailored research and consulting services based on your actual requirements, to give you an unparalleled service. Our locality, our experience and our proffesional know-how ensure your satisfaction. With over 10 years experience and 300+ clients, we believe that long term partnerships are the most successful means of entering the Turkish market. For company formations, market research, business partner searches, finding customers and business administration services in Turkey and beyond, FMConsulting should be your first choice local partner.

Merc Global Group
Contact: M.Ali Merc, Managing Director
Fevzi Cakmak Sokak. No:30/15 Kizilay-Ankara Turkey

Phone: +903122303182
Fax: +903122303185
Email: mercglobal@biri.com.tr
Web: http://www.mercglobal.com.tr
Oil & Gas & Energy field & Site Support. Turkish manpower staffing & supplying. Project management and consulting engineering. Renewable Energy investment consulting. Real Estate project development and land searching foreign companies representing and consulting. Global manpower staffing & supplying. Oil & Gas Hr Training and certification. Preparing work & resident permits for foreigners pay rolling and office services for foreigners pay rolling and office services for foreigners camp preparing & management and catering.

Engineering Services
Merc Global Group
Contact: M.Ali Merc, Managing Director
Fevzi Cakmak Sokak. No:30/15 Kizilay-Ankara Turkey
Phone: +903122303182
Fax: +903122303185
Email: mercglobal@biri.com.tr
Web: http://www.mercglobal.com.tr
Oil & Gas & Energy field & Site Support. Turkish manpower staffing & supplying. Project management and consulting engineering. Renewable Energy investment consulting. Real Estate project development and land searching foreign companies representing and consulting. Global manpower staffing & supplying. Oil & Gas Hr Training and certification. Preparing work & resident permits for foreigners pay rolling and

office services for foreigners pay rolling and office services for foreigners camp preparing & management and catering.

Export Management

CS Business Management and Support Services
Contact: Cagatay Altunsoy, General Manager
Egs Business Park Zemin Kat No:70
Bakirkoy
Istanbul Turkey
Phone: +902124652215
Fax: +902124652216
Email: info@csy.com.tr
Web: http://csy.com.tr

CS is a consulting and business services company providing international business consulting, start-up, market and product launch, international sales, marketing and instant office services in Turkey.

Due to our extensive business experiences in Turkey and because of our background with diverse industries, our extensive relationships in politics and business, we are the professional partner for a successful Turkish market entry. In order to offer our customers compherensive services through synergy effects and to provide exceptional results, CS also formed strong partnerships with other professional service providers.

Due to this Synergy Alliance Partner Program our clients additionaly benefit from our exceptional combination of expertise, international experience and business connections, high level connections, high level connections through the effective use of global networks and the synergy of strong partnerships.

We would like to invite you as our client and partner to break new ground in Turkey by taking advantage of our years of experience, economic and political networks and effective partner strategies.

Foreign Market Consulting Ltd. Sti
Contact: Ozlem Ilica, Sales Manager
Sumer Korusu Evleri Kasimpati sokak No:25 Tarabya
Istanbul, 34457
Phone: +902123638055
Email: o.ilica@fmconsulting.info
Web: http://www.fmconsulting.info

FMConsulting, established in 1999, is an international consulting and service company located in Istanbul, specializing in strengthening the market position of our international clients in Turkey.We provide tailored research and consulting services based on your actual requirements, to give you an unparalleled service. Our locality, our experience and our proffesional know-how ensure your satisfaction. With over 10 years experience and 300+ clients, we believe that long term partnerships are the most successful means of entering the Turkish market. For company formations, market research, business partner searches, finding customers and business administration services in Turkey and beyond, FMConsulting should be your first choice local partner.

Hospitals, Clinics, and Health Services

EDS Consulting
Contact: Can Acarlar, President
Tunus Cad. Tunus Apt. 88-7 Kavaklidere-Ankara
Acarkent 10. Cad 55.Sok B816 Beykoz-Istanbul
Ankara-Istanbul Turkey
Phone: +905324511585
Fax: +903124688128
Email: can.acarlar@edsdevelopment.com
Web: http://www.edsdevelopment.com

EDS provide consultancy services to our clients mainly emphasis on power, energy, oil, gas, healthcare, real estate project developments. Companies also turn to EDS for assistance in large complex sales situations for sales strategy, commercial terms and conditions structuring, a transaction management. EDS is known for detailed research, extensive local contacts and indepth understanding of local requirements.

Human Resources

Boyden Global Executive Search
Contact: Ozlem Ergun, Managing Director
Akcam Sokak No:22A 4.Levent
Istanbul Turkey
Phone: +90-212-278-3900
Fax: +90-212-281-2967
Email: ozlem.ergun@boyden.com.tr
Web: http://www.boyden.com.tr/istanbul/

Founded in 1946. Boyden Global Executive Search was the first to focus entirely on retained executive search, and continues to be leader in the executive search industry. We are a "global community" of more than 65 offices in over 39 countries, staffed by managers with an intimate understanding of the nuance of their particular market. Boyden Istanbul was established in 1998 by Ozlem Ergun to fullfill the growing need for qualified executive talent in Istanbul.

Merc Global Group
Contact: M.Ali Merc, Managing Director
Fevzi Cakmak Sokak. No:30/15 Kizilay-Ankara Turkey
Phone: +903122303182
Fax: +903122303185
Email: mercglobal@biri.com.tr
Web: http://www.mercglobal.com.tr
Oil & Gas & Energy field & Site Support. Turkish manpower staffing & supplying. Project management and consulting engineering. Renewable Energy investment consulting. Real Estate project development and land searching foreign companies representing and consulting. Global manpower staffing & supplying. Oil & Gas Hr Training and certification. Preparing work & resident permits for foreigners pay rolling and office services for foreigners pay rolling and office services for foreigners camp preparing & management and catering.

Odgers Berndtson Turkey
Contact: Ayse Oztuna Bozoklar, Managing Partner
Macka Cad. Ralli Apt. No:37 Kat: 5
Teskivikiye

Istanbul, 34367 Turkey
Phone: 902122318878
Fax: 902122312306
Email: ayse.oztuna@odgersberndtson.com.tr
Web: http://www.odgersberndtson.com

As well as executive search services for Board-level, senior and mid-management, Odgers Berndtson Turkey also provides Executive Talent Appraisal, Assessment, Organizational Development & Human Asset & Business Culture Review services. Odgers Berndtson Turkey handles assignments for local and multinational clients throughout Turkey, as well as covering the Central Asian region.

OneWorld Consulting
Contact: Burcu Uydan, Administrator
Ayazaga Meydan Sokak. No:28 Beybi Giz Plaza Kat 27 Maslak
Istanbul Turkey
Phone: +90-212-335-6424
Fax: +90-212-335-2500
Email: burcu.uydan@oneworldconsulting.com
Web: http://www.oneworldconsulting.com

OneWorld Consulting delivers quality People solutions with energy, passion, knowledge and high ethical standards. Our clients include companies getting started in Turkey, as well as major firms such as Allianz, Borusan, Coca-Cola, Google, Lafarge, Sabanci, Siemens, Unilever and Vodafone. We have also successfully completed projects in North Africa, the Middle East and Central Asia. We have a track record of delivering on challenging and sensitive search projects which make the most of our research, candidate handling skills and consulting experience.

Legal Services

Akinci Law Office
Contact: Mark D. Skilling, Attorney
Bebek Mah. Selcuk Sok. No: 4 Akinci Binasi
Bebek-Istanbul Turkey
Phone: +902122870700/ +90-533-642-4929
Fax: +902122878786
Email: mskilling@akincilaw.com
Web: http://www.akincilaw.com
Akinci's core competency is International Arbitration. Global Arbitration Review, for example, honored Akinci by picking it as one of its top 100 approved law firms worldwide, and the only one from Turkey. We also have solid corporate, labor and litigation departments. Quite a bit of our experience, in all area, is with construction matters. We have also developed, uniquely, considerable expertise in international family law matters.

Albayrak & Arslan
Contact: Ramazan Arslan, Partner-Attorney at Law
Phone: +902125575000 / +905325010362
Fax: +902125575002
Email: rarslan@albayrakarslan.com
The Law firm of Albayrak & Arslan was founded through the merger of two well established and respected legal practices. Understanding the potential offered by increasing commercial relationships with neighboring countries, our firm focused on a

strong international imprint from the very beginning. Today we have a client base of more than 500 companies, entrepreneurs and families who have used our legal services.Our firm's practice covers all corporate and commercial law areas, howevery Albayrak & Arslan differentiates from other local law firms in the legal consultancy services we offer to both national and international firms in the field of Business Establishment , Merger & Acquisition, Greenfield investment, Privatization, Project Finance, Restructuring & Insolvency, Employement, and Intellectual Property. Moreover, our firm is able to deliver investment services to companies seeking market entry in Turkey through our sistem company , Albars Consulting. For client matters that require advocacy outside of Turkey, the firm includes attorneys licensed to practice in the United States (Mr.Ramazan Arslan is admitted to both New York and Istanbul Bar Associations) and various European countries. Because of this jurisdictional versatility, we have become a preferred legal counselor for establishing and structuring large-scale international invesment projects.

Aydas Liman Kurman Attorneys at Law
Contact: Altan Liman, Mr.
Bestekar sokak 86/12 Kavaklidere
Ankara Turkey
Phone: +903124666662
Fax: +903124673331
Email: altan@aydaslimankurman.av.tr
Web: http://www.aydaslimankurman.av.tr
Aydas Liman Kurman is a full service law firm located in Ankara, aiming to provide high quality legal services to Turkish

and Foreign companies, governmental agencies and financial institutions as well as foreign and Turkish real persons. All members of the firm are fluent in English. Spanish and German are also spoken in the firm. Main practice areas of the firm are Banking and Finance Law, Company/Corporate Law, Commercial Law, Competition Law, Construction Law, Contracts Law, Environmental Law, Family Law, Direct Foreign Investments Law, Intellectual Property Law, Litigation,Pharmaceuticals and Healthcare Law, and Real Estate Law.

Babacan Law Office and Legal Consulting
Contact: H. Hare Babacan, Attorney at Law
Tunali Hilmi Cad. No: 89/77
Kavaklidere
Ankara Turkey
Phone: +903124661313
Fax: +903124661313
Email: hare@harebabacan.av.tr
Web: http://www.harebabacan.av.tr

Babacan Law Office is located in Kavaklidere-Ankara, which is very close to the US Embassy in Ankara. We specialize and dominate in civil and judicial cases. In addition we are providing consulting work and assistance to various domestic and international companies and organizations.

Our main mission is to protect, respect and fight for our customers's legal rights the fastest way while honoring our customers's requirements. This process is always accomplished under the strict guidance of domestic and international law rules.

Our law office is constantly following the latest changes and updates occuring in the world of law, in order to provide our customers with the most efficient legal solutions to their legal disputes.

Birsel Law Offices
Contact: Elif Acarlar, PA to Begum Durukan Ozaydin
Inonu Caddesi No:43 Ongan Apt Kat:4
Gumussuyu
Istanbul, 34437 Turkey
Phone: +902122455015
Fax: +902122455025
Email: elifacarlar@birsel.com
Web: http://www.birsel.com
Birsel Law Offices is one of the Turkey's oldest and most prestigious firms, and has a strong pedigree in all aspects of law, particulary in matters relating to banking & finance and mergers & acquisitions. The firm's partners, Mahmut T Birsel and Begum Durukan Ozaydin are very well regarded.

Eselioglu Law Office
Contact: Serhat Eskiyoruk, (LLB,LLB,PhD cn,MCIArb)
Turhan Cemal Beriker Bulv. Colakoglu Is Merkezi Kat 7
Adana Turkey
Phone: +903223523200
Fax: +903223521118
Email: eselioglu@eselioglu.av.tr
Web: http://www.eselioglu.av.tr

Eselioglu Law Office is a full service law firm with more than 40 years of experience. Eselioglu is based in Adana and has a contact office in Istanbul.

Debt Collection.

Foreign Market Consulting Ltd. Sti
Contact: Ozlem Ilica, Sales Manager
Sumer Korusu Evleri Kasimpati sokak No:25 Tarabya
Istanbul, 34457
Phone: +902123638055
Email: o.ilica@fmconsulting.info
Web: http://www.fmconsulting.info
FMConsulting, established in 1999, is an international consulting and service company located in Istanbul, specializing in strengthening the market position of our international clients in Turkey. We provide tailored research and consulting services based on your actual requirements, to give you an unparalleled service. Our locality, our experience and our proffesional know-how ensure your satisfaction. With over 10 years experience and 300+ clients, we believe that long term partnerships are the most successful means of entering the Turkish market. For company formations, market research, business partner searches, finding customers and business administration services in Turkey and beyond, FMConsulting should be your first choice local partner.

GSI Meridian Attorneys and Counselors
Contact: Ayfer Vural, Dr.
Suleyman Seba Cad. Besiktas Plaza B-Blok Kat:7
Akaretler-Istanbul, 34355 Turkey

Phone: +90-212-381-8067
Fax: +90-212-381-8048
Email: avural@gsimerdian.com
Web: http://www.gsimeridian.com

GSI Meridian is one of the top legal consultancy firms in Turkey, offering a wide range of legal services to both local and international clients regarding domestic and cross border transactions. Our areas of legal practice include energy, competition, real estate, corporate and M&A, privatization, taxation, intellectual property, capital markets, banking and finance, employment and labor, and litigation and dispute resolution, with a special focus on the telecommunications, financial services, media and broadcasting, and energy and natural resources sectors.

Guven Law Office
Contact: Selim Guven, Partner
Ataturk Caddesi 152/606
Izmir Turkey
Phone: +902324835551
Fax: +902324891972
Email: selim.guven@guven.av.tr
Web: http://www.guven.av.tr

Guven Law Office, with its experience of forty years offers legal services to regional, national and international corporations and real persons and aims to assist its clients and resolve their disputes in the best and most efficient way upon the Turkish Law System.

Law Offices of Koray Ayvali

Contact: Koray Ayvali, Principal Larry White, of Counsel
Hirfanli Sok. 12/5
Gaziosmanpasa
Ankara Turkey
Phone: +90-312-437-3875
Fax: +90-312-437-3827
Email: info@korayayvali.av.tr
Web: http://www.korayayvali.av.tr
The Law offices of Koray Ayvali is a full-service law firm in Ankara.

Nurdeniz Tuncer Law
Contact: Nurdeniz Tuncer, Lawyer
Rihtim Cad. Rasimpasa Mah. Nemizade Sok.
Karakuyu Apt. Kat:3 D:7 Kadikoy
Istanbul Turkey
Phone: +902164505627/+90532-541-4935
Fax: +902163481515
Email: info@nurdeniztuncer.av.tr/nurdeniz1@hotmail.com
Web: http://www.nurdeniztuncer.av.tr
The Nurdeniz Tuncer Law Firm is a private legal consultancy operating in Kadıköy on the Anatolian side and Beşiktaş on the European side of Istanbul. The firm was founded by Nurdeniz Tuncer who has been working as a private practicing attorney in Istanbul since 2004. Nurdeniz graduated from the Istanbul University Faculty of Law in 2001 and has received various certificates in the US.

Our firm specializes in commercial and financial law and services. Our assistance is available 24/7 in English and Turkish.

No matter what the time zone difference is, or where you are in the world, you can rest assured that you will be able to get prompt service from our team when you need it. Here at the Nurdeniz Tuncer Law Firm we help foreign and Turkish clients navigate the legal and financial proceedings of Turkey without frustrating confusion or uncertainty. We are prepared to represent and serve a variety of clients in financial consulting and commercial and contract law.

Our financial advisor Ozan Fulser, here at the Nurdeniz Tuncer Law Firm is ready to assist you in any financial proceedings you will be concerned with in the future or are currently involved in. We can help you expand your business into Turkey, sell your company, or deal with Turkey's tax law. We have a great deal of experience in financial consulting, and can assist you in mergers, acquisitions, financing, project finance, stock offerings, loans and lending, and any other local or cross-border financial transactions.

In addition to these financial consulting services we can help you deal with any other legal issues or business needs related to your industry locally and internationally, and are able to give counsel in construction, real estate, customs, energy law, Organized Industry Zones legislation, intellectual property law, dispute resolution, privatizations, unfair competition and antitrust actions, and other areas of commercial law.

We are equally comfortable with domestic and international proceedings. Whether you are a large company or an individual we can help you be successful here in Turkey and we want to represent you. We offer an unprecedented level of personal support and attention, with our firm you can sleep easy knowing that we are working for you and are available for any questions or concerns you have.

Yalcin Law & Consultancy Office
Contact: Sertac Yalcin, Attorney at Law
Güneş Sk. No:16/3 Kavaklıdere Çankaya/ANKARA
Phone: +903124404889
Fax: +903124404899
Email: sertacyalcin@yalcinhukuk.com
Web: http://www.yalcinhukuk.com
Our legal Office, practices and offers comprehensive specialist advice in the fields of national and international law.

Market Research
CS Business Management and Support Services
Contact: Cagatay Altunsoy, General Manager
Egs Business Park Zemin Kat No:70
Bakirkoy
Istanbul Turkey
Phone: +902124652215
Fax: +902124652216
Email: info@csy.com.tr
Web: http://csy.com.tr
CS is a consulting and business services company providing international business consulting, start-up, market and product launch, international sales, marketing and instant office services in Turkey.

Due to our extensive business experiences in Turkey and because of our background with diverse industries, our extensive relationships in politics and business, we are the professional partner for a successful Turkish market entry. In order to offer our customers compherensive services through synergy effects and to provide exceptional results, CS also formed strong partnerships with other professional service providers.

Due to this Synergy Alliance Partner Program our clients additionaly benefit from our exceptional combination of expertise, international experience and business connections, high level connections, high level connections through the effective use of global networks and the synergy of strong partnerships.

We would like to invite you as our client and partner to break new ground in Turkey by taking advantage of our years of experience, economic and political networks and effective partner strategies.

Foreign Market Consulting Ltd. Sti
Contact: Ozlem Ilica, Sales Manager
Sumer Korusu Evleri Kasimpati sokak No:25 Tarabya
Istanbul, 34457
Phone: +902123638055
Email: o.ilica@fmconsulting.info
Web: http://www.fmconsulting.info

FMConsulting, established in 1999, is an international consulting and service company located in Istanbul, specializing in strengthening the market position of our international clients in Turkey. We provide tailored research and consulting services based on your actual requirements, to give you an unparalleled service. Our locality, our experience and our proffesional know-how ensure your satisfaction. With over 10 years experience and 300+ clients, we believe that long term partnerships are the most successful means of entering the Turkish market. For company formations, market research, business partner searches, finding customers and business administration services in Turkey and beyond, FMConsulting should be your first choice local partner.

Marketing, Public Relations, and Sales
CS Business Management and Support Services
Contact: Cagatay Altunsoy, General Manager
Egs Business Park Zemin Kat No:70
Bakirkoy
Istanbul Turkey
Phone: +902124652215
Fax: +902124652216
Email: info@csy.com.tr
Web: http://csy.com.tr

CS is a consulting and business services company providing international business consulting, start-up, market and product launch, international sales, marketing and instant office services in Turkey.

Due to our extensive business experiences in Turkey and because of our background with diverse industries, our extensive relationships in politics and business, we are the professional partner for a successful Turkish market entry. In order to offer our customers compherensive services through synergy effects and to provide exceptional results, CS also formed strong partnerships with other professional service providers.

Due to this Synergy Alliance Partner Program our clients additionaly benefit from our exceptional combination of expertise, international experience and business connections, high level connections, high level connections through the effective use of global networks and the synergy of strong partnerships.

We would like to invite you as our client and partner to break new ground in Turkey by taking advantage of our years of experience, economic and political networks and effective partner strategies.

Foreign Market Consulting Ltd. Sti
Contact: Ozlem Ilica, Sales Manager
Sumer Korusu Evleri Kasimpati sokak No:25 Tarabya
Istanbul, 34457
Phone: +902123638055
Email: o.ilica@fmconsulting.info
Web: http://www.fmconsulting.info
FMConsulting, established in 1999, is an international consulting and service company located in Istanbul, specializing in strengthening the market position of our international clients in Turkey.We provide tailored research and consulting services

based on your actual requirements, to give you an unparalleled service. Our locality, our experience and our proffesional know-how ensure your satisfaction. With over 10 years experience and 300+ clients, we believe that long term partnerships are the most successful means of entering the Turkish market. For company formations, market research, business partner searches, finding customers and business administration services in Turkey and beyond, FMConsulting should be your first choice local partner.

Mining, Oil, and Gas Services
EDS Consulting

Contact: Can Acarlar, President

Tunus Cad. Tunus Apt. 88-7 Kavaklidere-Ankara

Acarkent 10. Cad 55.Sok B816 Beykoz-Istanbul

Ankara-Istanbul Turkey

Phone: +905324511585

Fax: +903124688128

Email: can.acarlar@edsdevelopment.com

Web: http://www.edsdevelopment.com

EDS provide consultancy services to our clients mainly emphasis on power, energy, oil, gas, healthcare, real estate project developments. Companies also turn to EDS for assistance in large complex sales situations for sales strategy, commercial terms and conditions structuring, a transaction management. EDS is known for detailed research, extensive local contacts and indepth understanding of local requirements.

Real Estate Services

Antalya Homes Real Estate
Contact: Ahmet Tigli, Sales Manager
Barınaklar Bulvarı 5/5 07230 Lara
Antalya Turkey
Phone: +902423245494
Fax: +902423241830
Email: info@antalyahomes.com
Web: http://www.antalyahomes.com
Leading real estate company is based in Antalya with 2 offices. Company is specialized in residential property sales to international property buyers in Lara, Konyaaltı, Alanya, Belek and Kemer. There are 8 different languages spoken at Antalya Homes office.

Purchasing your dream property from Antalya Homes gives you the privilege to benefit from our exclusive "before and after sales" services. All property offers has a due-dilligence report ready.

EDS Consulting
Contact: Can Acarlar, President
Tunus Cad. Tunus Apt. 88-7 Kavaklidere-Ankara
Acarkent 10. Cad 55.Sok B816 Beykoz-Istanbul
Ankara-Istanbul Turkey
Phone: +905324511585
Fax: +903124688128
Email: can.acarlar@edsdevelopment.com
Web: http://www.edsdevelopment.com
EDS provide consultancy services to our clients mainly emphasis on power, energy , oil, gas, healthcare, real estate project

developments. Companies also turn to EDS for assistance in large complex sales situations for sales strategy, commercial terms and conditions structuring, a transaction management. EDS is known for detailed research, extensive local contacts and indepth understanding of local requirements.

Spot Blue Overseas Property Ltd.
Contact: Julian Walker, Manager
Link House, 140 The Broadway, Surbiton, Surrey, Ktg 7Ht
United Kingdom
Phone: +4402083396036
Fax: +4402083396168
Email: info@spotblue.co.uk
Web: http://www.spotblue.co.uk

Spot Blue is a leading Anglo Turkish specialist real estate agent helping international buyers find and purchase their villas, apartments or land in Turkey. Spot Blue has many years of experience offering European standards to the Turkish property buying process and a safe and secure way of finding and owning property or land in Turkey. Spot Blue has English and Turkish representatives in all the most popular Turkish locations.

Turyap Yapi San. ve Tic. A.S
Contact: Ayse Serbes, Assistant General Manager
19 Mayis Caddesi Dr. Ismet Ozturk Sok.
Sisli Plaza Ofis Bloklari E Blok Sisli
Istanbul Turkey
Phone: +90-212-373-1300
Fax: +90-212-380-2290

Email: aserbes@turyap.com.tr
Web: http://www.turyap.com.tr

Turyap is the first franchising organization of real estate business in Turkey. It is carrying on a business real estate marketing sector with 380 agencies and 1500 personnel in 43 cities. It conducts its activities with real estate actions, special projects, real estate barter and integrated building management. TURYAP currently carries on the printing and publishing of Emlak Pazari journal which consists over 2000 real estates for sale & rental ads, and is sold all over the country with a circulation of 13.000.

Translation and Interpretation

Enterkon
Contact: Selma Ogan, International Coordinator
Ayaspasa Cami Sok. No:4 D:2 Muge Apt. 34437 Gumussuyu Istanbul
Phone: +90-212-249-5249
Fax: +90-212-249-1938
Email: enterkon@enterkon.com.tr
Web: http://www.enterkon.com.tr

Enterkon, the leading interpretation company of Turkey, was established in 1987 as the first commercial organization in the field. Its core activities are simultaneous, consecutive and whispering interpretation as well as high-quality translation services with our competent translators and editors. Enterkon - www.enterkon.com.tr has built a well-deserved reputation as a reliable partner thanks to its professional secretariat and competent team of interpreters who are members of AIIC(www.aiic.com) and TKTD (www.tktd.org). Enterkon is proud to serve governments, international organizations and multinational companies.

UKT Uluslararasi Konferans Tercumanlari A.S.

Contact: Israk Aydemir, Coordinator

Mutevellicesme Sokak Pinar Apt. A Blok 42/A Daire:8

Kosuyolu- Uskudar/ ISTANBUL

Phone: +90-216-418-6604

Fax: +90-216-450-5046

Email: ukt@ukt.com.tr

Web: http://www.ukt.com.tr

UKT International Conference Interpreters has an experienced and reliable team of interpreters working in English- French- German- Russian- Turkish and Italian. Our interpreters are members of AIIC (International Association of Conference Interpreters) and BKTD (Turkish Association of Conference Interpreters).

The Internationalist

www.internationalist.com

www.ingramcontent.com/pod-product-compliance
Lightning Source LLC
Chambersburg PA
CBHW051727170526
45167CB00002B/826